'This original text presents an innovative interdisciplinary approach, where key concepts within different paradigms – such as jouissance in Lacanian theory, surplus value in Marxist theory, and nothingness/emptiness in the Buddhist tradition – relate to each other, challenging the boundaries of traditional political theory, and inviting us to rethink the relations among power, ethics, and civil society.'

**Martin Hopenhayn**, *Social theorist for United Nations; author,* Beyond Nihilism and the Sense of Belonging in Fragmented Societies

# Lacan, Jouissance, and the Social Sciences

Exploring how a Freudian-Lacanian approach to psychoanalysis intersects with social and cultural theory, *Lacan, Jouissance, and the Social Sciences* demonstrates the significance of subjectivity as a concept for the study of leadership, social psychology, culture, and political theory.

Raul Moncayo examines Lacan's notion of surplus jouissance in relation to four types of socio-economic value: Productive Value, Exchange Value, Surplus Value, and Profit. Also drawing on the work of Slavoj Žižek, Moncayo contends that surplus production cannot be reduced to alienated labor but rather includes various levels of jouissance-value. In this way, the jouissance that drives capitalization and organization can be theorized as constructive rather than destructive and encompass satisfaction and prosperity rather than individual suffering and asceticism or living with less.

This volume will be of great interest to psychoanalysts both in practice and in training and to academics and scholars of psychoanalytic studies, Lacanian studies, and social sciences.

**Raul Moncayo, PhD**, is a supervising analyst and a founding member and past president of the Lacanian School of Psychoanalysis, USA. Dr. Moncayo was also the training director of a large psychiatric clinic for many years in San Francisco. In 2022 he founded The Chinese American Center for Freudian and Lacanian Analysis and Research. He has been an adjunct faculty and a visiting professor both locally and abroad and is the author of 11 books.

# Routledge Focus on Mental Health

Routledge Focus on Mental Health presents short books on current topics, linking in with cutting-edge research and practice.

# Lacan, Jouissance, and the Social Sciences
## The One and the Many

**Raul Moncayo**

Routledge
Taylor & Francis Group

LONDON AND NEW YORK

First published 2023
by Routledge
4 Park Square, Milton Park, Abingdon, Oxon OX14 4RN

and by Routledge
605 Third Avenue, New York, NY 10158

*Routledge is an imprint of the Taylor & Francis Group, an informa business*

*British Library Cataloguing-in-Publication Data*
A catalogue record for this book is available from the British Library

*Library of Congress Cataloging-in-Publication Data*
Names: Moncayo, Raul, author.
Title: Lacan, jouissance and the social sciences : the one and the many /
Raul Moncayo.
Description: Abingdon, Oxon ; New York, NY : Routledge, 2024. |
Series: Routledge focus on mental health | Includes bibliographical references
and index. |
Identifiers: LCCN 2023017558 (print) | LCCN 2023017559 (ebook) |
ISBN 9781032515977 (hardback) | ISBN 9781032515946 (paperback) |
ISBN 9781003403012 (ebook)
Subjects: LCSH: Social sciences and psychoanalysis. | Psychoanalysis and
culture. | Surplus value. | Pleasure. | Lacan, Jacques, 1901-1981.
Classification: LCC BF175.4.S65 M635 2024 (print) | LCC BF175.4.S65
(ebook) | DDC 150.19/5—dc23/eng/20230501
LC record available at https://lccn.loc.gov/2023017558
LC ebook record available at https://lccn.loc.gov/2023017559

ISBN: 9781032515977 (hbk)
ISBN: 9781032515946 (pbk)
ISBN: 9781003403012 (ebk)

DOI: 10.4324/9781003403012

Typeset in Times New Roman
by codeMantra

This book is dedicated to John Dewey, Roberto Harari, Guillermo Estefan, and the Wright Institute for knowing how to read the pulse of the social sciences so well. It is also dedicated to all high school philosophy teachers to whom the responsibility falls to synthesize the knowledge of the culture for its youth.

# Contents

# Introduction

This book will explore the psychoanalytic categories that contain many useful elements that intersect with elements of social and cultural theory. We all know that psychoanalysis is a vital blood vein running through the body of knowledge in the social sciences, and as such stimulates basic research. Psychoanalysis is the medium through which the branches of social science must pass, while it retains its own field of application outside the university.

The specific contribution of this book is to examine Lacan's notion of surplus jouissance as a form of social value, something that was previously done by Zizek (2022). However, this book is centered on Lacan's later notion of the three forms of the Third jouissance as a form of surplus value and surplus jouissance that is neither inconvenient nor destructive. The objective of social and cultural theory, according to Freud (1930), is to describe the achievements, principles, and cultural regulations that distinguish human culture from animal and biological life and instinct. This division is itself reproduced subjectively between the human and animal aspects of a human being.

The conflict between animals and humans is reproduced into a subjective conflict between humans and their ideals whether secular or religious. The ideals and perfect satisfaction are never reached because sublimation does not eliminate the lack. Both sexual pleasure and sublimation don't eliminate the lack but sublimation does not reproduce it or intensify the suffering associated with it. Freud believed that religion led not to an increase but a decrease of happiness due to the guilt associated with religion that increases suffering and despair due to a fear of the religious super ego installed in the human ever since the primal horde and the erection of the first totem.

In a nutshell, this book represents a Freudian-Lacanian approach to the social sciences that concedes a central role to subjectivity as a legitimate approach to the study of leadership, primate research, social psychology, culture, and political theory. However, this is no panpsychicism or a psychoanalytic caricature of how political forms or events could be reduced to biographical data or a pan politicism of how psychic events could be understood politically or are intrinsically political in nature.

DOI: 10.4324/9781003403012-1

Primatologists go from the state of group psychology and social life of subhuman primates to the evolution of trade and economic relations in humans, skipping altogether how the process of symbolization and symbolic exchange took place in the leap from primates to humans, from the biological order to the symbolic order. Primatologists pretend and hope Freud did not exist or said nothing about human evolution.

For Freud and Lacan, the early form of the signifier originally represented the death or killing of an animal, an enemy, or the leader of the group. The totem represents the taboo placed upon the community for the deed and the taboo or prohibition placed upon the leaders not to be like the primal father. The totem itself is the mark of the unmarked and the background upon which the mark is written. The totem represents the ritual killing of a totem animal that came to replace human sacrifice in the form of the killing of the enemy, the father, or the leader. In fact, the totem itself is a mark of the unmarked killing of the father and subsequently used to mark the killings of the totem animal.

The bull and the ox became a totem animal that represented both the dead father and the totem animal. The metaphor of the sacrifice and symbolic castration of the bull that then is known as an ox that pulls the cart and plough, at the heart of the development of agriculture, is itself an allegory of the father-son relationship. In the Jewish Midrash, Jacob the father is the cart (the vehicle) and Joseph the son the ox. The ox and the symbolic castration of the bull is an image of the throne of glory in which G-d sits and represents the sacrament and good deed of circumcision. G-d's throne has an ox in its north corner. The temple in Jerusalem also has an ox in its north corner. Joseph was pulling the yoke of his father to plow the future of the Jewish people and humanity.

Psychoanalytic theory most beautifully links areas of knowledge that may have seemed hitherto unrelated (biological anthropology and evolution, religion, social psychology, literature, etc.). Aside from utilizing concepts from across the social sciences and from conceptual mathematics, this book's formula for symbolic castration and its application to a formula for culture is an example of a concept that links separate fields of knowledge.

Political theory in this book does not refer to party politics but to theory in a more post-structural sense that includes the intensities of jouissance (See the Glossary at the end for a definition of jouissance) representative of Lacan's later work. The Symbolic Other is not the same as the political Other. The Symbolic Other and repression for psychoanalysis must exist in any society regardless of its political structure. Emancipation refers to freedom from the unnecessary or pathological aspects of "surplus repression" as Marcuse (1955) called it. One may want to change structures of domination in history, but this is not the same as undoing the necessity for the law or the establishment of healthy forms of repression and self-discipline such as those associated with the incest prohibition in the family.

Herein lies the ambiguity of psychoanalysis for the study of society. Is a body politic comprised of a nursery with babies who cannot rule themselves and must be ruled by nurses, so it is inevitable that the society will contain a ruling class or government and a ruled class or people? This is where the Freudian left confuses ordinary repression with oppression or social surplus repression. In addition, subjectivity is not imaginary or fantasized subjectivism the same way that introspection is not psychoanalysis. Subjective fantasy also has a logic that must be understood symbolically and with the objectivity of language and the signifier.

The function of psychoanalysis for social and cultural theory instead is to clarify the register and status of the specific jouissance involved in symbolic and economic objects of exchange, in consumption and production, and in the excess that drives the capitalization and organization of the system, for the Other and the subject. We follow Freud when he extends the conceptual "formulas of psychoanalysis" regarding the joint of nature and culture, to the joint of psychoanalysis and the social sciences where the latter may benefit from psychoanalytic theory and practice.

Freud (1930) began his famous essay on Civilization and its Discontents by commenting that people seek power, success, and wealth for themselves; admire them in others; and underestimate what is the true value in life according to him. There may be differences in what the true value of life means for different people. For some the true value is family, for others the true value is pleasure or sexuality, for others the true value is found in physical or martial culture, for others the true value is spirituality and community, for others the true value is science and knowledge, etc.

Thus, for example, advocates of material values may or may not support family values but in general support community values. Power, success, and wealth are material values that Freud considers suspect or untrue, yet even though Freud was a scientific materialist, his views, nonetheless, coincide with the Chan Buddhist or spiritual definition of worldly success, power, wealth, and domination, as vain pursuits. However, Chan focuses on everyday secular life and equally avoids vain material pursuits and ascetic withdrawal from the ordinary world. Chan Buddhism is not religion in this sense, while psychoanalysis is not simply materialistic. There is something beyond material and spiritual that unites them.

Symbolizing the material body with spiritual values is not a killing of the drives or the body since such "imprisonment" of the body is a generative aspect of the death drive. The conflict is not that of a rider or ruler and a horse or ruled. Bodhisattvas ride untamed elephants. The empty spirit of the word enhances and beautifies and frees the body rather than destroy it. Otherwise, it would be the case of a deadly spirit destroying itself.

Idols were prior gods who included a practice of self-scourging or self-laceration with knives to consecrate themselves to the mother as a form of self-emasculation. The presence of the gods instead of making people better make them weak and sickly.

(Heschel 1962a, p.211)

But if the death drive is bent on destroying itself, how could it have constructive functions within the Real and the Symbolic. This is the misunderstanding between nothingness and emptiness, between the First and Third jouissance, and between a dual absence of something or an object and the non-dual presence of emptiness as "something" (energy) both in the absence and presence of the object.

Freud thinks that the intensity of the meditation state or Nirvana is not as satisfying as the intensity of sexual satisfaction. Sex momentarily extinguishes the lack but then intensifies the clinging to the object and the subjective experience of lack, while sublimation also provides a satisfaction that stops the repetitive search for the lost object but does not lead to clinging to the object or reinforce an experience of the lack as a form of deficit. Freud expressed the hope that one day the joy experienced by a scientist could be understood and conceptualized in Metapsychological terms. This is precisely what I believe to have developed, thanks to Lacan, with the use of the concept of the Third jouissance.

A psychoanalyst, however, never practices politics or takes explicit political points of view with analysands. In addition, although Freud and Lacan had much to say about the origins and nature of society and culture, both could be said to be *a*political in the sense that their writings and seminars do not endorse a particular political orientation (Roazen, 1968, p.242). Some have interpreted Freud as having an elitist political bias much like Socrates and Plato did.

In Seminar XXIII (2015) Lacan says that a quality of the sinthome (homophony with *saint homme* or holy man) and of the analyst is to be separated from politics. In the traversal of the fantasy ($\$\diamond a$), the ideal ego and the ego ideal are transformed. In the "matheme" for the ideal ego (i[a]) and the ego ideal (I[A]), the *i* [ego] separates from the *a* [*objet a*], and the I [ideal] separates from the A [Other]).

Nowhere did Freud and Lacan advocate violence as a solution to any problem, something that distinguishes them from the Freudian and Lacanian left. In fact, Freud was rather pessimistic about human nature precisely due to the violence and devastation he witnessed in World War II. War is a form of barbarism that strips us of civilization. Freud did not think there were such a thing as an ethical war.

Nor am I trying to extrapolate from analytical practice to treat society or the political system as the analysand, for the same reasons that it is questionable to comment on a biography if that person has not been the writer's analysand. Citizens should not be treated as patients that can be convinced that their resentments concerning the political order are grounded in purely private or personal difficulties. Although rebellions may turn out to be regressive, citizens have the right to introduce changes into their government.

In this sense, this book does not represent applied psychoanalysis either. Psychoanalytic theory can be applied to analytic practice but can also be used for other purposes, so long as the pure theory that determines what we call psychoanalysis is based on its practice. The theory then can be utilized by other fields to develop their own fields. This book is focused on how psychoanalysis theorizes the joint between nature and culture, and since this joint is also the joint between psychoanalysis and the social sciences, social and cultural theory may benefit from Freudian and Lacanian concepts.

This book uses psychoanalytic categories for the elucidation of social theory, not only because of the historical import of Freud's thought for Judeo-Greek-Christian civilization but because Freud encompasses both Hobbes' (1651) and Locke's (1681) theories of government in his understanding of how biological animal instinct function in evolution, together with how a culture, as a different second form of nature, that structures the human natural environment, interacts with biology and evolution. Freud famously wrote works on society and culture: Civilization and its Discontents, Totem and Taboo, and the Future of an Illusion. Freud's theory is deeply rooted in Western intellectual history, even though, Totem and Taboo, for example, was received as containing not truth but fiction. Lacan would say Totem and Taboo contains truths within a fictional structure.

Freud agrees with both thinkers in the theory of the social contract but more with Hobbes in the appraisal of animal instincts and their manifestation within human beings. I also think we are justified in using psychoanalytic principles, since, as Locke indicates, childhood family environments, or the "paternal metaphor" as Lacan calls it, lead to better governments and societies.

I use Freud and Lacan to understand the theory of government not to take a political position for or against a particular ideological configuration of power. In addition, the power of domination is not the only true form of power. Truth and practical reason are more than techne. Heaven, the Dao, Dharma, Torah, or Gospel, or the register of the spirit of the word, and that of virtual fantasy are more than material reality (they are psychical reality) and represent the emptiness within form and its possibilities.

For these causal reasons, the theory does not translate into a relative political action plan but rather focuses on the true principles and fantasies that may underpin political systems of various kinds given local circumstances. The assumption is that what one may lose by not linking the theory to an emancipatory political practice and what one gains by understanding which symbolic frameworks may maximize the possibility of re-thinking the notion of human emancipation.

Social theory that includes symbolic and fantasized logical relations cannot be left purely within the realm of ideology or reduced to relations of power and domination, or to hiding, rather than revealing, conditions of domination. Language, cultural forms and structures, and the law are not simply Imaginary or cover over the truth of rapacious relations of domination. Truth is more than domination, although relations of domination must be understood as true. The true is not Truth. The Symbolic is not Ideology or the Imaginary but rather represents the structural conditions for productive symbolic exchange.

In his theory of moral sentiments, Adam Smith (1759) showed that our moral ideas and actions are a product of our very nature as social creatures. Here moral ideas would evolve from the life of the group in evolution. However, Smith does not consider the leap from the ape to the human in terms of the appearance of symbolic life, language, and culture.

For Smith like for Freud and even perhaps (1859), the facts of our nature as social creatures represented psychological realities that were not necessarily rational yet capable of being understood rationally. For Smith and Freud social psychology is a better guide to moral action than reason. As social creatures we are all endowed with a natural empathy towards others. Such natural kindness we have understood and found already in subhuman primates. But just because kindness is part of biological life and evolution, it does not mean it has to be understood irrationally.

I distinguish between the unknown, the unknowable, and rationality of various kinds. The unknown is the rational yet unknown, and the unknowable is what cannot be understood by progressive layers of words, numbers, and jouissance. Emptiness and compassion are concepts that are not concepts but placeholders for something consistent with reason but beyond reason at the same time. The layers of rationality I have discussed elsewhere (Moncayo, 2021), including Nous which as a form of reason represents an unconscious form of intuition.

Simple or evolved compassion also has a quality of restraint over anger and other intense emotional reactions that may not be acceptable to other people, especially those representing the values of the culture. Although the emotional reactions of the ego may not be acceptable to the other, the subject is more than the ego. The defenses are the calming defenses of symbolization and the empty mirror of mind that is also the source of non-sentimental compassion. The empty mirror of mind reflects the other as they are, while also sharing the empty mirror with the other. As we grow from childhood to adulthood, we each learn what is and is not acceptable or unpleasant to society. Instead of opposing society with individualism and ego-drives, the subject of the signifier and of the Real leads to a cultural subject with a capacity to reign-in destructive drives. Morality stems from our social nature that itself depends on the quality of the ancient mirror of mind that sustains the social bond and reflects reality as it is.

The mirror is a natural element that does not rely on a socially imposed duty for compassion although the latter reinforces the former. In the ancient and ancestral mirror of mind and nature, everything is the cause of everything else, and at the same time, the source of causality itself is acausal or empty. Finally, Smith regards freedom and nature as non-rational principles because he does not utilize the Aristotelean practical reason, nor how the irrational can be explained by rational and irrational numbers, Nous as a form of reason, and a theory of jouissance.

For Keynes (1935), economic decisions are intuitive, emotional, and irrational. People tend to reach irrational conclusions about money, and this has been called the "money illusion" or money as a fetishistic commodity or object of worship. But expectations of profit or success surprisingly are not the only animal factor affecting confidence in economic activity.

Perceptions of fairness, or the human spirit, are also a crucial factor in financial decisions. Fairness means equal access to the risks of gains and losses that the market and life afford us. In fact, those who succeed do so because of the ability to withstand failure and use failure not to obscure but realize a vision.

The function of culture is to teach subjects how to succeed despite failure. Loss is necessary for success. Fairness is linked to the function of culture of regulating the drives and the animal spirits resulting in some form of self-discipline. However, the regulation is also itself an index of jouissance that transforms the function of the drive into a different form of capitalization and jouissance. If unregulated, the drives and capital (Akerloff and Schiller, 2009) become a form of inconvenient excess and accumulation which is destructive to the society because it leads to an increasing gap in income distribution.

The normal psychical losses of the subject in the family and their elaborations prepare the subject to procure the gains and sustain the losses afforded by social goods and objects of consumption. This I argue is what Keynes referred to as animal spirits in the marketplace. The use value or the labor value of the object is not its jouissance value that cannot be measured in real numbers. Jouissance value is measured in imaginary and complex numbers. A complex number carries both the real number and value of labor invested in an object and the added or surplus jouissance as an imaginary number added to the real number. In Lacanian theory, there are different forms of surplus jouissance, and by the same token, the type of satisfaction experienced with an object may vary.

The theory propounded in this book may be equally helpful to One Party or Two-Party systems, as examples of two democratic political systems. In this sense, this book does not agree with Fukuyama's (1992) thesis that liberal capitalism represents the final successful system in history. This book avoids ideological dichotomies such as between autocracy and democracy or between liberal and socially focused democracies. For example, the Taiwan problem can be easily resolved over time with the One China policy, since Chinese culture includes Chinese Chan Buddhism which encourages the peaceful resolution of conflict. In addition, 90% of the Taiwan population favor maintaining the One China policy that has equally benefitted both countries. What this book argues about democracy would apply equally to both.

Finally, taking the step of seeking political power and office necessarily involves the Machiavellian political imaginary unless politicians are trained in advance to serve the people rather than their own self interests.

Both capitalism and socialism are incomplete systems that harbor an unprovable true contradiction that holds the consistency of the respective system together.

1  Socialism and capitalism contradict each other because the needs of the people in society may contradict the interest of capital and its necessary social taxation.
2  Capitalism and democracy contradict each other because the needs of capital call for restrictions on democracy when it interferes with the interests of capital or because capital introduces factual, non-representative powers that interfere with a democratic processing of decisions.
3  Socialism and democracy may contradict each other given that socialism calls for a restriction and restraint placed on the individual, and if there are enough individuals who feel frustrated in their rights and aspirations, this will create a contradiction between socialism and democracy.

A functional definition of democracy requires a correct definition of the relationship between the individual or the subject and the Other of society. Democracy includes the methods we use to arrive at decisions, but the decisions themselves must strike an accord between the One and the Many, realize the common good, and not be diverted or influenced by considerations of power or personal economic profit.

When the interest of the Many do not contradict the interest of the subject of the Real defined outside the Many, such definition of a self, that is a no-self that cannot be proven, then reinforces the consistency of a system/structure that benefits the interests of the Many. Although the One or the Real is outside the Many, or the Symbolic, the One is still within the Borromean structure that contains both the Many and what lies outside the Symbolic. The true self that is a no-self that cannot be proven is a slender trace of the Third jouissance of the sinthome that holds together the Borromean structure of the knot of four.

## References

Akerloff, G. and Schiller, R (2009). *Animal Spirits: How Human Psychology Drives the Economy, and Why It Matters for Global Capitalism*. New Jersey: Princeton University Press.

Darwin, C. (1959). *On the Origin of Species by Means of Natural Selection, or the Preservation of Favorite Races in the Struggle for Life*. New York: D. Appleton and Company.

Freud, S. (1930). *Civilization and its Discontents*. New York: Norton 1961.

Fukuyama, F. (1992). *The End of History and the Last Man*. New York: Free Press.

Heschel, A. (1962a). *The Prophets*. Volume I. New York: Harper & Row Publishers.

Hobbes, T. (1651). *Leviathan*. New York: Collier Books, 1962.

Keynes, J.M. (1935). *The General Theory of Employment, Interest and Money*. Cambridge: Macmillan Cambridge University Press

Lacan, J. (1975–1976). *The Sinthome*. London: Polity Pres.

Locke, J. (1681). *Two Treatises of Government*. The Project Gutenberg EBook of Second Treatise of Government by John Locke.

Marcuse, H. (1955). *Eros and Civilization*. Boston: Beacon Press.

Moncayo, R. (2021). *The Practice of Lacanian Psychoanalysis*. London: Routledge.

Roazen, P. (1968). *Freud: Political and Social Thought*. New York: Alfred Knopf.

Smith, A. (1759). *The Theory of Moral Sentiments*. Adansonia Press, 2018.

Zizek, S. (2022). *Surplus-Enjoyment. A Guide for the Non-Perplexed*. London: Bloomsbury Publishing.

# 1 The Primal Horde of Primates and Early Humans

For this section I will review what we know thus far about the social and mental organization of primates and their evolution into early humans.

Before there were tribes of hunter-gatherers and aboriginal societies, let alone a Greek polis, there was a primal horde of human beings derived from subhuman primate hordes. Hordes are typically reproduction units aimed at the reproduction of the individual and the mating groups. In monkeys, copulation outside the hormonal cycle of the female is relatively rare. Males are never significantly involved in raising the young. Primate groups develop from initial promiscuity to the establishment of exclusive sex partnerships that become the nucleus of the primate horde. In the beginning, the only stable relations are between females and their young.

During the menstrual cycle females become attached to several specific males in succession. Dominant males have all the females (2–11 in the case of baboons) in the menstrual cycle, while subordinate males are excluded if there are not enough females left over for them. In this case, subordinate males are excluded from sexual relations with females. Males are usually in conflict over females in their hormonal cycle. Weak and sick males are attacked. The more intelligent chimpanzees, however, show "friendly or benevolent dominance". Subordinates are protected rather than attacked. Dominance and prestige become associated with the service of the group.

The temperance of dominance relations is continued in the forms of social organization of primitive human hordes. Since cooperative teamwork requires symbolization, which they don't have, monkeys are not capable of organized social cooperation. Sharing food, for example, is only one way: from subordinates to dominant monkeys who never share their food. Food sharing and pooling of resources became a characteristic of the human horde. Food cooperation replaced the search for sexual mates. Leadership by a dominant male now has to display qualities of intelligence, thinking, and generosity and an ability to resolve conflicts among the horde.

Primatologists go from this state of affairs to trade and economic relations, skipping altogether how the process of symbolization and symbolic exchange took place in the leap from primates to humans, from the biological order to

DOI: 10.4324/9781003403012-2

the symbolic order. The rules of exogamy and incest prevent the formation of the family on the basis of sexual attraction. Subsistence of the species in culture becomes more important than copulation. Sexuality has come under social control, used for other ends. As we see, a quick survey of the contemporary research on subhuman primates reveals several of the features that Freud, following Darwin (1859), described in the transition from the primate horde to the primal human horde. A quick survey of the field shows the evidence of the crime: a complete denial of Freud's genius.

Nowadays anthropological knowledge seems normal and scientific, but in Freud's time to say that anything like the prohibition of incest existed in normal society would be shocking and widely condemned because, of course, how could Freud be so morally depraved to think that parents and children had sexual fantasies about each other. Freud was regarded as a perverse Jew and was condemned for proposing that the prohibition of incest, the castration complex, and Oedipal structure were all linked to the structure of human society, human sexuality, and reproduction, and relations between the sexes. What we did to Freud, we cannot forget.

Since even the prohibition of incest was not enough to account for his theory of normal incestual sexual wishes, Freud had to go to great lengths to explain that a prohibition would not be erected for something that was not there already. This is like when people say that rules in communities only become necessary once conflicts break out between people, or natural propensities emerge that require the intervention of others and the culture. In fact, the "external" intervention is already a repetition of structural laws built into the system of symbolic exchange that were there already in the first place.

Following structural anthropology, Lacan argued after Freud that prohibition or law and desire emerge together. The prohibition or symbolic castration creates lack and desire, and desire longs after a forbidden object, fruit, or agalma. Symbolic castration civilizes phallic sexuality and the aggressivity between men because, as Freud (1927a, b) remarked, sexual desire divides rather than unites men. What I (Moncayo, 2015) have called the formula for symbolic castration is built into the function of culture, or culture is built around a phallic function of symbolic castration, that requires that every subject gives something of themselves to become a citizen.

The offering of the "pound of flesh" is what is meant by the socially certified use of the masculine phallus. The use of the phallus requires a loss, in the same way that, for the feminine sex, the phallus and themselves "appear" inexistent. However, this loss is also an indication of jouissance and of transformations within jouissance. The Lacanian proposition regarding the inexistence of femininity refers to how femininity "ex-sists" in the Real, rather than saying that femininity does not exist in a primitive binary sense. The inexistence of a woman refers to how the objet a dissolves in its approach to the Real.

In his famous study on *Totem and Taboo*, Freud (1913) described the taboo on eating animals as the nucleus of Totemism. Taboos emerge from primordial prohibitions that represent the psychological determinants of the taboo. Freud notes a scientific step-by-step correspondence (correlation not causality?) between the record of taboo usages and modern obsessional symptoms. Or are obsessional symptoms (determined effects/affects) vestiges of taboo usages? Taboo usages involve the body but are primarily cultural symbolic forms, and the same can be said about neurotic symptoms: both need to be understood through the medium of language and symbolization.

There is no doubt that taboo practices existed and still do nowadays, but what is not so easy to determine is the origin of taboo prohibitions. Freud believed that the prohibition was originally imposed by an external authority. But since he could not prove or demonstrate such primordial deed, he seeks its vestiges in the correspondences between modern disorders and archaic cultural forms.

Genetic mutations, or past cultural forms, in the course of evolution and history leave behind certain characteristics that may become the basis for the development of illness and psychopathology. Mutations not only produce evolution but also cause illnesses. Conversely, viruses associated with illnesses could also be mutated into new life forms within gene structure.

In *Totem and Taboo*, Freud follows not only Darwin's primate observations but also what was known then about the transition from the primate horde to the human horde, to then what became known as savage or aboriginal society. The terms savage refers to the violence of nature and to the natural instincts that have been controlled under human civilization.

However, the term savage, the notion of an archaic and primitive mentality, and the lineal notion of cultural development or progress from animism to religion, to science, were severely questioned during the twentieth century in anthropology, psychology, and political theory. Early humans both desire and are afraid of violating taboos and prohibitions. Taboos are erected to handle the ambivalence towards the leader and to regulate reproduction, sex, and kinship relations.

## References

Darwin, C. (1859). *The Origin of the Species*. London: Nmd Books.

Freud, S. (1913). *Totem and Taboo*. SE 13, 1–161.

Freud, S. (1927a). *The Future of an Illusion*. SE, Vol. 21.

Freud, S. (1927b). *Civilization and Its Discontents*. SE, Vol. 21.

Moncayo, R. (2015). *The Real Jouissance of Uncountable Numbers*. London: Karnac.

# 2 The Primordial History of Symbolic Exchange

Chapter 1 surveyed contemporary research on subhuman primates that revealed several of the features that Freud, following Darwin, described in the transition from the primate horde to the primal human horde. However, I also note some differences. What Freud recognized as a primal feeling of ambivalence (once the hatred was satisfied, the feeling of love for the father re-emerged), more recent primatologists (Goodal, 2001, and de Waal, 2009) have noted that the alpha male has prestige (and not only force, an early form of legitimacy) in the group, what I described above as friendly dominance (benevolent dictator) because he also protects them and helps them with their quarrels. Kindness is a natural feeling that is socialized by transforming hate into its opposite. The love they felt for the father led to guilt and to the erection of the totem. They could preserve themselves by uniting their common power and purpose in the figure of the totem. This is first covenant and social contract. First, humans lose their natural freedom but discover a more valuable social freedom under totemic law.

Subhuman animals and a primal human horde, thereafter, also feel love towards the leader of the group. The first leader of humans, not historically or phylogenetically but ontologically for the individual, is the mother in the first group of two (dyad). However, Freud saw that every child at the breast repeats the pre-historical relationship to the primal father. A dyad is already a group as Freud and Lacan said. In every mother-child relation, or a group of two, there is a third in the form of the primal father, the father of the child, and the mother's own father. "The hypnotic relation is (if the suggestion is permissible) a group formation with two members" (Freud, 1921, p.115).

By the same token, every father is a father in a family by virtue of the paternal function or metaphor that includes the mother's desire. The father is pre-figured in the mother's desire, and, therefore, it makes sense that the primitive or archaic first love and hate towards the mother's breast (ontogenetically) would repeat the same towards the imaginary phallus linked to the primal father (phylogenetically). The hate towards the breast refers to how one of the breasts represents frustration or when the breast is not available, while the hate towards the father refers to how the father represents symbolic

DOI: 10.4324/9781003403012-3

and imaginary castration. What is lost in frustration and castration according to Lacan is one of the logical forms of the *objet a* cause of desire.

Separation from the objects of desire and the mother is the beginning of frustration and socialization into a human group. The separation from the breast and the mother marks the beginning of symbolization as a continued step in the temperance of dominance relations that begun with the primal horde.

The early form of the signifier originally represented the death or killing of an animal, an enemy, or the leader of the group. The totem represents the taboo placed upon the community for the deed and the taboo or prohibition placed upon the leaders not to be like the primal father. The totem itself is the mark of the unmarked and the background upon which the mark is written. The totem represents the ritual killing of a totem animal that came to replace human sacrifice in the form of the killing of the enemy, the father, or the leader. In fact, the totem itself is a mark of the unmarked killing of the father and subsequently used to mark the killings of the totem animal.

What I (2015) have called the formula for symbolic castration is built into the function of culture, or culture is built around a phallic function of symbolic castration, that requires that every subject gives something of themselves to become a member of society.

The offering of the "pound of flesh" (Shakespeare's *The Merchant of Venice*'s metaphor for social circumcision) is what is meant by the socially certified use of the masculine phallus. The use of the phallus requires a loss, in the same way that, for the feminine sex, the phallus and themselves "appear" inexistent. However, this loss is also an indication of jouissance and of transformations within jouissance. The Lacanian proposition regarding the inexistence of femininity refers to how femininity "ex-sists" in the Real, rather than saying that femininity does not exist in a primitive binary sense. The inexistence of a woman refers to how the *objet a* dissolve in its approach to the Real.

## References

De Waal, F. (2009). *The Age of Empathy*. New York: Harmony Books.
Goodal, J. (2001). *The Chimpanzees I Love*. New York: Scholastic Press.
Moncayo, R. (2015). *The Real Jouissance of Uncountable Numbers*. London: Karnac.

# 3 Benevolent Tyranny and Love as a Motive for Repression

Freud states that the motives of the taboo prohibition are unconscious and that they are maintained by automatic and repetitive forms of mental organization. For example, forbidden natural and cultural objects have a magical and repressed quality that threatens to infect and invade the subject because they become associated with a forbidden deed or a primal sacrifice. Freud (1913) gives the example of the taboo upon leaders, given that a chief or a king occupies the position of the primal father later replaced and represented by the totem. Many objects associated with the chief also acquire a magical and foreboding quality that threatens to infect and invade the subject because they have become unconsciously associated with a forbidden deed or a primal sacrifice.

> "The king or chief arouses envy on account of his privileges: everyone, perhaps, would like to be a King". A subject, who dreads the great temptation presented to him by contact with the king, can perhaps tolerate dealings with an official whom he does not need to envy so much and whose position may seem attainable to him.
>
> (1913, p. 33)

A subject dreads contact with the chief not only for the prohibition he/she represents but because of the murderous envy that could lead the subject to transgress the prohibitions. Taboo rituals and reactions simultaneously express both tendencies. For these reasons, rulers were both protected from the people and guarded against. This is an intrinsic aspect of the ambivalence of the group or the Many towards the One or the leader. At the same time, the chief or leader resents all the restrictions placed upon them by the group and from which other people are exempt, in order to deserve or be entitled to their privilege. Leadership is both a blessing and a curse, to the point that leaders may pose serious resistance to being invested with any form of official public authority. In fact, Mencius said about Confucius that just as it was necessary to assume political office to help the people, it was equally necessary to leave as soon as a suitable replacement for the leader has been found.

DOI: 10.4324/9781003403012-4

This is the subjective and structural basis for a social democracy. Washington relinquished power after two terms in power to establish a democracy, and Confucius left because he did not want power and wanted to avoid the primitive archaic group processes, and I guess for his own safety.

Freud further notes that the same remarkable ambivalence is shown towards enemies. It is not surprising that enemies are hated. What is surprising to find in the so-called savages is that after the enemy is killed or even eaten, the enemy is also loved, and the attacker feels remorse and grief over what they did. Such remorse and expiation are partly felt and partly performed to appease the spirit of the dead.

Psychoanalytic theory, given the familiarity with unconscious process, and psychopathology allow us to easily advance from describing social events such as these, to explaining how the hatred towards the leader is transferred to the enemy, and how the proof of such transference, is that after the enemy is killed, a similar feeling of love and loss emerges towards the enemy that is felt towards the leader. This kind of behavior may be more "civilized" than more recent treatment afforded to enemies. Although, in consciousness, love and hate are directed to different objects, the mind preserves an unconscious link between love and hate that is revealed when either love or hate has prevailed.

In addition, although the leader is perceived as powerful and even omnipotent, the leader is also vulnerable and needs to be protected from the people. The people typically don't trust the leader with the use of power. This is the origin of the principle that the leader must be under the same law or power that is exercised upon subjects. Psychoanalytic theory would simply explain this by the principle that the leader or the father also needs to be under the formula for symbolic castration as the principle for social organization.

Ultimately the formula for symbolic castration is how symbolization and temperance of dominance relations is achieved. There is consistency between sexuality coming under cultural control and given new aims, rather than ends, as Freud would say in his theory on the sexual drive. The aim is still within the drive, while ends in this case refers to purposive or axiological ends layered on top of the drive. The sexual instinct became a symbolic drive in human beings. In humans, animal instinct is both revealed and repressed, articulated, and disarticulated by cultural principles.

Freud supposed that both the primate and the first human horde were led by the bigger and more dominant male in the group. I said above that primate studies show that dominant males have all the females (2-11 females each in the case of baboons) in the menstrual cycle, while subordinate males are excluded if there are not enough females left over for them. In this case, subordinate males are excluded from sexual relations with females. Males are usually in conflict over females in their hormonal cycle. Weak and sick animals are attacked.

These are the essential ingredients of Freud's formulation of the first human group, with a few notable exceptions discussed below. The primal ape was brutal, had all the women, and subordinated all the men, including his sons. Conversely, the sons were also brutal and wished to destroy the father's social standing. The females also seek to reproduce with the primal ape. Along the lines of Hobbes theory and social contract theory, Freud sees the conspiracy to band together and kill and eat the father, as an indication of the struggle to the death of all against all.

Since the sons also love the father, once they kill him two things happen: one is that, due to the love of the father, they experience remorse, and two, they soon realize that they will repeat the entire process again with each other, and, therefore, they renounce violence and place a totem or a totem animal in lieu of the murdered and cannibalized father. The totem is the first signifier of the father and the beginning of symbolization and language in this account. The $S_1$ of the totem replaces the murder of the father and exalts the father at the same time.

The question of the father's love is interesting because it opens the question of whether Freud's account is complete (not that it could ever be in every respect). I mentioned above that chimpanzees show friendly dominance, and this observation has also been reported by Jane Goodall in her field studies of gorillas. When the alpha male showed his territorial dominance by pounding his chest, she simply "acted" or performed submissiveness without the humiliating sting of dominance or imaginary castration and slowly approached the gorilla. The alpha male let her sit next to him and held her hand. This is an example of how subordinates are protected rather than attacked.

The alpha male has prestige in the group because he also protects them and helps them with their quarrels. Animals capacity for love has also been amply demonstrated, and therefore, it is not surprising how subhuman animals and a primal human horde could also feel love towards the leader of the group. This is so much the case that Freud believed that every nursing infant revisits the ambivalence towards the primal father in the obvious surface love the infant experiences for the mother's breast. Ambivalent love appears in the normal infant rages because of inevitable frustrations and the fantasized destruction of the breast.

The separation from the breast and the mother marks the beginning of symbolization as a continued step in the temperance of dominance relations that begun with the primal horde. I said that since cooperative teamwork requires symbolization, which monkeys don't have, monkeys are not capable of organized social cooperation. It is in the relationship of attachment and separation to the primary food source and its symbolization that cooperative teamwork becomes possible in humans. The fusion and separation to the primary food source is already mediated by the leadership of a dominant male that now must display qualities of intelligence, thinking, and generosity and an ability to resolve conflicts among the horde.

The separation from the primary food source and the biological mother in humans is also regulated by the rules of exogamy and incest that prevent the formation of the family based on sexual attraction. Subsistence of the species in culture is more important than copulation. Sexuality has come under social control, used for other ends. As we see, a quick survey of the contemporary research on subhuman primates reveals several of the features that Freud, following Darwin, described in the transition from the primate horde to the primal human horde.

In the human horde, symbolization begun in the form of the unary mark.

The unary numeral system is the simplest numeral system to represent natural numbers. In order to represent the concept of number, an arbitrary notch, stroke, trait, trace, vertical bar, or a tally mark written "|" or "/" is repeated N times. For example, using the tally mark "|", the number 4 is represented as "||||"." … Nowadays, of course, humans are not using strokes or marks but natural numbers to count things (like adding apples to oranges, or counting the number of people attending a lecture, or counting the number of deaths in a region at a certain time). As per Jottkandt (2010, p.24) "the ability to count reaches into the heart of identification because it is the original and simplest form of evidence that a subject has successfully understood and become able to use a system of symbolic representation." The first appearance of it was for primitive people to keep a tally of killed animals by making marks on ribbon, a piece of material, or the bark of a tree.

(Moncayo, 2015)

The early form of the signifier originally represented the death or killing of an animal, an enemy, or the leader of the group. The totem represents the taboo placed upon the community for the deed, as well as the taboo or prohibition placed upon the leaders not to be like the primal father. The totem itself is the mark of the unmarked and the background upon which the mark is written. The totem represents the ritual killing of a totem animal that came to replace human sacrifice in the form of the killing of the enemy, the father, or the leader. In fact, the totem itself is a mark of the unmarked killing of the father and subsequently used to mark the killings of the totem animal.

The killing of a totem animal, and its marks, and the ability to count, also came to be associated with money in the same way that a coin came to be represented as a magical object or a magical property mark of the king. The coin would represent the king as well as the totem or the deity behind the power of the king. The power of the deity comes from the sacrificial act itself, that is reexperienced in its full ambivalence in relation to the leader and his magical signs and objects.

From the mark follows the Name of the totem and of the clan that also stands for the Name of the Father. The Name at this point is not linked to a cultural or ideological $S_2$, only to the totem body, and this remains structurally true to this day. The Name represents the kinship with the animal, the totem, and the father. From here follows that before the "hunter/food-gatherers" period of human culture and evolution, there were early humans out of which the first symbol arose to represent the killing not of an animal but of the primal father. This is Freud's hypothesis (myth) that I endorse and re-present to you.

As the totem replaced the primal father, the totem and the totem animal eventually became identified with the bull and the cow, and the bull became identified with a king, father, or deity. It became important to sacrificially kill them since such a killing would legitimize a system of exchange, where the cow and the bull could be used for their productive value as milk, meat, labor, and ritual entertainment. The ritual provided a validation for a system of symbolic exchange where eventually cattle became a unit of value in ancient times and marks could be used to count them. *Capitale* originally designated counting cattle by the marks on their heads and bodies (Borneman, 1976). For the Babylonians the bull was a god (Baal) that was replaced by the ox that symbolizes the yoke of the heavens, the symbolic castration and submission of Jacob the son to the father for the good of the generations.

The killing of the totem animal not only validates the internal coherence of the culture but also validates a system of economic exchange with outside clans or groups. Surplus animals are given over to the totem deity. Over time, the excess is used to exchange other goods with neighboring groups. The production and reproduction of surplus animals, at this point, does not represent unnecessary labor since many needed goods are exchanged for the totem animal.

Finally, I mentioned that the figure of a loved father and a feared and hated enemy coincided in the figure of the primal father. The love towards the father led to the renunciation of parricide and infanticide, and the fear of the living and dead father was displaced towards the totem and the totem animal. The totem had an awesome and dreaded aura that included both the power of the deed and the power of the renunciation that the totem represents. Ambivalence is continued in relation to the totem and the totem animal. The totem is to be not only engaged but also avoided, just as the leader. The fear of the father leads to phobias towards objects that are considered sinister, impure in any way, or to have a contagious magic, poison, or disease. This is how coins and money came to be associated with feces, anality, and the father as the enemy or devil.

## References

Borneman, E. (1915). *The Psychoanalysis of Money*. New York: Urizen Books, 1976.

Freud, S. (1913). *Totem and Taboo*. SE 13.

Moncayo, R. (2015). *The Real Jouissance of Uncountable Numbers*. London: Karnac.

# 4 The Group

At this point, an interesting paradox emerges regarding Weber's (1958) thesis about the origins of capitalism in Protestantism. Luther is stuck with having to negotiate his salvation with the devil in the figure of the merchant as the only place that salvation can be won. The protestant surrenders to the acquisition of money and paying taxes as a divine calling. To take up the cross meant to assume the burden of work and earning money. Eventually, money loses its association with the work of evangelizing the devil and the world (in G-d we trust) and regresses instead, according to some (Brown, 1959; Fromm, 1966), to its earlier links with something evil to be avoided such as an idol or devil worship (the fetishism of commodities). However, the so-called irrationality of money may not be irrational in the ordinary sense, I argue, and instead may be organized by the so-called irrational numbers that form part of number theory as a rational construct.

The distinction between imaginary and real numbers also points to a distinction between surplus production based on constructive versus destructive forms of jouissance. Only compulsive unnecessary labor can be linked to destructive forms of surplus jouissance. For Marxist theory, the production of a surplus disturbs the criterion of what is necessary and instead performs a surplus and compulsive unnecessary labor.

Other Lacanian readings (Zizek, 1989) of capitalism primarily utilize Lacan's first conception of the Real and jouissance to represent surplus capitalist value as something excessive in the sense of an inconvenient obscene form of jouissance of the Other that may represent suffering more than pleasure. Zizek's analysis of ideology incorporates the analysis of the fantasy into the fabric of social reality itself.

The conception of the Real in Seminar XXIII (Lacan, 1975) is different, since the Real is duplicated, and the new Real features a constructive Third jouissance that makes accord and ties a new form of the Borromean knot. From the vantage point of this new theory, the jouissance that drives the capitalization and organization of the system can be theorized as constructive rather than simply destructive.

DOI: 10.4324/9781003403012-5

Lacan's second Real is a true empty hole and a form of jouissance that is organizing of structure, whether it be social, political, or mental. In this way, Lacanian theory answers Freud's questions regarding the Eros that creates ever larger unities. This is not sexuality, since sex divides as much as unites, and is not a form of de-sexualization but a direct manifestation of the drive as Freud ambiguously held. Unity and conformity with the order are forged in ties of love not on economic and political interests.

Lacan definition and use of the term accord should not be confused with Deleuze's use of the same. Deleuze (Parr, 2010) calls capital the accord of accords par excellence. However, Deleuze's concept is philosophical, while Freud's analysis of money is anthropological, social, and psychological at once. We trace money to early marks and forms of counting, and in this sense capital simply represents the accord signified by the first totem. The accord in this case is not based on values, narratives, or ideologies. The agreement or contract is based on individual psychical factors and also operative in the group mind. This establishes the rule of the Symbolic over the Imaginary and the Real.

Agreements supersede natural inclinations and now regulate biological reproduction. The Real changes from the unspeakable trauma of parricide and death to the mana and power assigned to the totem and the principle of symbolization. Eventually, the repressed inclinations and the power of the Real prove to be too much for the symbolic organization to contain, and a new knot needs to be created. Out of the second form of the Real, a new knot of four needs to be generated. I argue that Deleuze mistakes the ideological unity of the Imaginary with the Real. Precisely because the One of the Real is defined by the One's own non-being, the One of the Real can be mistaken for the One of the Imaginary. The One of the Real that is not in conflict with the Symbolic, but rather gives it its structure, can tie a knot of four that will hold the dimensions in place.

Finally, I have previously defined three forms of love in RSI (Moncayo, 2022). The love that forges unbreakable bonds is not imaginary love or infatuation with a leader or an idea (imaginary love). Remember that Freud considered the state of being in love the normal prototype of psychosis. Nor is it only a question to commitment to a practice (symbolic love, in marriage or partnership). In the previous book, I wrote about the three forms of love according to the three registers; however, I omitted to mention Lacan's comments on Seminar XX. There he says that symbolic love aims at Being. Wanting to be loved is a demand that the Other give us our Being that we cannot find in ourselves. Instead, the One of the Real unconsciously gives us a surprise rather than our Being. The Being of Being cannot be found in the Other due to the One's own non-being. We are seeking for the One in the Real rather than Being as the only way to reach being in emptiness.

Love in the Real is love for the lack and inexistence of the Other. But here lack means both, an absence in the sense of a symbolic poverty of self, a humility combined with generosity, the lack in the mother and the father, and the transiency of beauty itself.

## References

Brown, N. (1959). *Life against Death. The Psychoanalytical Meaning of History.* Middletown, CT: Wesleyan University Press.

Fromm, E. (1966). *You Shall Be as Gods.* New York: Holt, Rinehart, and Winston.

Lacan, J. (1975). *The Sinthome. The Seminar of Jacques Lacan.* Book XXIII. Cambridge: Polity Press.

Moncayo, R. (2022). *The Practice of Lacanian Psychoanalysis.* London: Palgrave.

Parr, A. (2010). *The Deleuze Dictionary.* Edinburgh: Edinburgh University Press.

Weber, M. (1958). *The Protestant Ethic and the Spirit of Capitalism.* New York: Scribner & Sons.

Zizek, S. (1989). *The Sublime Object of Ideology.* London: Verso.

# 5    The Polis

There are two views of how the first villages were formed. The first village, town, city, or fortification was military when a scattered group of nomads or hunter-gatherers came to live in one city behind a set of protective walls. The second view of the polis is political: a group of people agreed to live under one authority, with or without the protection of a walled city (Ryan, 2012). The early example of the Harappa people of the Indus Valley Civilization provides an alternative example where cities may have been organized non-hierarchically and under collective or chosen authority. However, scholars are divided about this or there is not enough evidence to decide one way or another. Of course, this statement of how the polis begun sounds extremely naïve in the light of everything that was said above about the primate and human horde. This is an example of how scientific specialization is counterproductive.

As villages began to be organized into larger cities with larger economies and systems of cultural exchange, these also needed to be protected with larger defensive structures and more complex value systems. Human settlements have been found that go back 12,000 years (Gobekli Tepi in Turkey including the oldest temple in the world) using farming to provide a surplus that could be stored for future use (communal storage) or used as object of exchange. They worshiped a headless dead subject, the bull, and an erect phallus, suggestive of Freud's (1913) myth of the primal father or the symbolic castration required for the social use of the phallus and the totem as a sign of culture's human culture ascendancy over nature in evolution. According to some, Gobekli Tepi shows evidence that religion led to agriculture and farming rather than the other way around. The infrastructure would have its origins in the superstructure, providing evidence for Weber's ideas.

The first village of hunter-gatherers, as a scattered group of nomads, would seem to be the beginning of a human social organization beyond the primate group and beyond the primal human horde. How did humans' transition from a primitive social organization to a social organization based on rational and symbolic principles?

The first step would be to bind sexual and aggressive impulses of individuals that threaten to destroy the cohesion of the social group. In the primal

DOI: 10.4324/9781003403012-6

horde, such repression was achieved by the ambivalent love feelings towards the father or group leader. The love for a cruel leader asserted itself in the restitution of the murdered father/leader in the form of the sublated totem that henceforward functions as principle of unity and social cohesion and peace between the siblings and members of a group. Aggressiveness and rejection of the totemic principle from then on are regarded as unjustified and destructive of social organization. Rejection of the justified and legitimate authority of the totem now is seen as a form of unjustified selfish form of individualism, even though the action may have originated from instinctual animal behavior.

Cultural developments in Greece, China (Lao zi and Confucius or Kong zi), and Israel (Hebrew prophets, Heschel 1962, ab) also led to an organized thought about political life in the city around 11,500 later (500 BC). This in turn led to the creation of new technologies for construction, roads, buildings, etc. In the end, the argument between Marx (1872) and Weber (1920/1958) is circular: infrastructure and superstructure mutually determine each other.

Rational thought and wisdom about good government represents a first step in binding sexual and aggressive impulses to dominate others that threaten to destroy the cohesion of the social group. The first principle is either the principle of the self-will to dominate others (government of "real men" according to Machiavelli) or the totem that signifies an acceptance and affirmation of the symbolic order (government of laws) and the spirit and Name of the dead father ruling over the group. Confucius and Aristotle presuppose a secular harmony in nature that intends us to live a good life in common.

Aristotle (1912) gave the world an early definition of different types of government that have withstood the test of time and history. For Aristotle, the bad, irrational, or instinctual forms of government were the tyranny of the wealthy few or oligarchy, the tyranny of an unethical majority or mob, and the tyranny of a dictator or monarch without a constitution or representative government and ruling only on behalf of their own selfish interests. A constitutional monarch as such only exists nowadays as a monarch that adheres to the constitution and accedes not to political power but to a symbolic or presidential position that oversees the principles of civility and security upon which the political order is based.

This differs from a theocracy where the monarch is both ruler and priest, where the monarch has both worldly and spiritual power, and where both can be corrupted by each other. This form of theocracy would also have to be defined as a bad form of government according to Aristotelean definitions especially when the crafting of a constitution is not done by a deliberative representative body representing people but also using various forms of expertise and points of view. This form of deliberation may also take place within a One or Two-party system.

According to Freudian principles, bad government comes to existence because of the ambiguity leftover from the transitional leap from animal nature to human nature. The totem is the first symbol of good government and the beginning of nature as culture and symbolization. From then on, the totem or second nature will pre-exist the individual in its natural form prior to socialization. The question that follows and remains is how does the totem include the sweetness of human nature that according to Aristotle and Confucius (1938) leads to the good social life?

The totem represents a form of sublimation and transformation of the animal into the human although sweetness and kindness already exist in animal nature contrary to what Freud believed. Freud observed that the sons felt remorse over the murder and eating of the primal father because in the end, they realized that they also loved him. Their hate was "lovehating" as Lacan calls it. Human culture and rational principles of organization are also built on predispositions found in animals linked to their capacity to cooperate and help each other. The totem stops murder at the point of maximum pressure of the drive and not only when the animal is satiated and capable of cooperation without aggression. This in my opinion answers the question of how extreme aggression came under human control (Wrangham, 2019) thanks to the totem and the events of the primal horde.

Without principles of law and justice arising from the totemic principle, humans could become even more evil and destructive than similar actions observed in animals. A man with weapons or technology and without principles is the most unholy and savage of all the animals and the worst regarding sexual indulgence and gluttony.

Democracy is not the rule of pure license or freedom from the law that eventually ends up in tyranny. For this reason, Socrates, Plato, and Aristotle rejected democracy defined in this way. The book defines Justice and the Law, whether natural, human, or divine, as what re-signifies the order of animal nature within human beings. Driven by the survival of the fittest, most animals attack the weaker members, while symbolic justice and Law are based on a kindness towards the vulnerable members of a species. Freedom within a democratic society represents the laws that allow us to live the best life in common as human beings.

Justice and a constitution must also protect the interests of talented individuals assigned by nature. Talent may come from any class and not only from the wealthy. Talent represents the interests of the individual that are geared towards the common collective good and therefore should be supported rather than rejected. Justice equally prevents that equality degenerates into negative equality or egalitarianism and that talent degenerates into individualistic activities that do not benefit the Many.

Intellectual and spiritual leaders, however, must choose their own spiritual successors (only talent can recognize talent in others) before leaders become confirmed by either vote or service to the people. Here we need to distinguish between political leaders and spiritual and intellectual leaders. As is often the case, the latter may help the former but do not hold political power or office. In political office, it is not only up to the leader to choose a successor. In intellectual or spiritual leadership, a leader organically chooses his or her successor based on the talent and chance factors assigned by nature. Successors, of course, must also prove themselves in relationship to the collectivity and the Other of society.

Representative democracy unites the common sense of the Many with the talent of the One. This is a universally valid form of government. Talent and meritocracy in principle are the best form of government: the best people rule in the service of the people because they possess judgment, courage, justice, and moderation in the highest degree. A democracy can also be measured by the question of social mobility. Can the middle class grow into the leadership class, and can the lower class grow into the middle class? In the cases that the working class becomes the ruling class, then the officers of the government become the middle class, and the people become either a rich upper class or a prosperous middle class. However, all this is held together by the cultural history of a nation which varies from nation to nation.

The Greeks were concerned with the motives that lead people to seek political power and took for granted that these are selfish motives, not unlike Lao zi or Kong zi in China, around the same time. Selfish motives are the same as the aggressiveness to dominate others, although such domination may also have had survival value for animal species. People much prefer to be bossed about others than to be bossed about themselves, and cultures that identify with this principle as a principle of the will, and the national will, will inevitably descend into authoritarianism and cruelty towards others. Initially, power is motivated by aggressiveness rather than justice, and the so-called justice is barely distinguishable from naked aggression. Socrates thought that the ambitions that drove most political leaders were a form of madness or a sickness of the soul. This perspective is entirely consistent with Darwin's and Freud's account of the male in the primal horde.

If justice is a quality in rulers, they should be concerned with the welfare of their subjects rather than themselves: justice promotes the interest of the weak, not the strong. But of course, this all depends on how we define strong and weak. If the interests of the strong or weak are ethical, then either group pursuing their interests is "justified". A just life makes strong or weak individuals stronger, while an unjust life makes the strong weak, and the weak or strong in the sense of becoming tyrannical or destructive.

If the tyranny of the majority or the weak is not ethically or rationally justified, then pursuing their interests does not result in Justice. Justice is also understood as the familiar value that leads humans to keep promises, tell the truth, do their duty, and obey the laws. Outside the realm of "criminal justice", social justice is defined in economic terms as a state's commitment to achieving some form of fairness in the economy.

Plato (2013) held that morality was inscribed in the natural order, and he despised the Sophist view that nature was amoral, that men were selfish by nature, and that law – nomos – was a matter of convention. Aristotle also claimed that the polis existed "by nature" because nature means us to live a good life in common.

> Now it has been said in our first discourses, 1 in which we determined the principles concerning household management and the control of slaves, that man is by nature a political animal; [20] and so even when men have no need of assistance from each other they nonetheless desire to live together. At the same time, they are also brought together by common interest, so far as each achieves a share of the good life. The good life then is the chief aim of society, collectively for both all its members and individually; but they also come together and maintain the political partnership for the sake of life merely, for doubtless there is some element of value contained even in the mere state of being alive, provided that there is not too great an excess on the side of the hardships of life, and it is clear that the mass of mankind cling to life at the cost of enduring much suffering, which shows that life contains some measure of well-being and of sweetness in its essential nature. (Aristotle, the Ethics).

Now what is the sweetness of our essential nature that wants us to live a good life in common? Does this mean that the good life is regulated by a life-preserving instinct? Self-preservation of the individual or the species is a chief good, and therefore, the growth of the city-state can be seen as a natural form of development. The original band of brothers acted out of self-preservation in eliminating the danger represented by the cruel and vicious primal father. At the same time their own destructiveness led to the killing of the primal father and this deed threatened to unleash a deadly war of all against all where the strongest and most dominant male would prevail, and the struggle would repeat itself all over again from one generation to the next. The erection of the totem put a stop to the compulsion to repeat the original crime between the group and its leader, the sons, and their father.

The totem group, or a group organized by totemic principles, is the first principle of a polis or of a city-state that pre-exists the individual in its natural state. The totem is the symbol of the One as the principle of a united form of social organization.

Aristotle thought that the impulse to form a social partnership and cooperation is present in all men by nature. However, this is not a form of goodness found in nature that does not need struggle and conflict for it to arise. Aristotle, as many others, thought that goodness was a quality found in rational leaders. However, how does virtue and rationality first arise in human beings? Darwin and Freud provide us with a materialistic and historical account of how virtue may have been born out of struggle, violence, and conflict.

The man or father who first united people was the greatest of benefactors but was not originally without asocial forms of instinctual dominion and destructiveness. The struggle that led to the father's humanization and transformation was not a struggle between good and evil inside the primal father but rather a struggle between father and sons where both equally represented good and evil impulses.

Without principles of law and justice arising from the totemic principle, humans could become even more evil and destructive than similar actions observed in animals. In addition, the invention of weapons made human even more dangerous than animals. Weapons and instruments discovered through human rationality must be legitimized and used for constructive social purposes lest they undo all human progress painstakingly achieved by prior generations. A man with weapons or technology and without principles is the most unholy and savage of all the animals and the worst regarding sexual indulgence and gluttony.

The totem is the first signifier and the beginning of symbolization and repression. The murdered father is brought back to life as a unifying social principle represented by the totem. The totem sublimates and represses aggressiveness towards the father. As we see, instinct is not a reliable foundation for the survival of society since instinct comes to conflict with the social symbolic order setup to regulate and sublate animal instincts.

Here an appeal to a pre-existent harmony of Nature, as found in Leibniz's philosophy, is not a satisfactory explanation because Nature can also be destructive of human culture. A harmonious immanence of Nature, as seen in pantheism or panentheism, or in Taoism, for example, can only be recovered through a human symbolic order and then not without difficulty and struggle. Quantum theory of a universe organized by a dialectic between Order and Chaos provides a better explanation.

However, human culture and rational principles of organization also rely on predispositions found in animals linked to their capacity to cooperate and help each other. Without appealing to a notion of divine love or harmony in nature and remaining within a scientific account of evolution, we have found in Freud's account and the results of primate research that kindness also appears spontaneously in nature.

Plato also rejected democracy as the rule of pure license or of a culture without prohibition, where everyone does just what they want, and the weakest or lowest point of the political cycle alienates the better-off in terms of talent, virtue, or meritocracy. Especially when powerful individuals are alienated, the remaining many may end up in tyranny rather than democracy. Tyranny is the worst of all possible governments. Plato's view of democracy as the rule of the mob or pure license led to his sweeping rejection of political life as not being much more than "ape shit" or the social organization of the primal horde.

Harming someone means making them worse, says Socrates, and the point of justice and Real love cannot be to make someone worse. Therefore, how are we to understand Socrates when he says that Justice is whatever is in the interest of the stronger? (The Republic-Book I). This may be understood as the claim that whoever gets to have the upper hand and be dominant and gets to define right and wrong as they please. The rich define the Law as preserving private property, as a human right, while the poor define the Law as what protects the poor from the whims of the rich. The definition of a human right differs in both cases. One is a human right to own what a citizen has obtained through legal efforts and work, while the second is the human right to not be inhumanly exploited.

When the Law is perceived as legitimate, and the rich as having a right to their possessions, then for the poor, justice represents a form of generosity to the rich and those in power that, nonetheless, leads them to act against their own self and class interests. They give of themselves because they are poor and remain by such behavior. The interests of the stronger here means the interests of those physically or technologically stronger, rather than those with stronger characters and merit. If justice is a quality in rulers, they should be concerned with the welfare of their subjects rather than themselves because justice promotes the interest of the weaker, not the stronger.

Justice, whether natural, human, or divine, is what re-signifies the order of animal nature within human beings. Driven by the survival of the fittest, or a misunderstood will to power, most animals attack the weaker members, while symbolic justice is based on a kindness towards the lack in the Other that protects the vulnerable members of a species.

Writing 2000 years later, in the aftermath of the English Civil War, Hobbes (1651), who translated Thucydides and was himself deeply hostile to democracy, made the revolutionary claim that we are by nature equal, not unequal. But equal here means the ability to destroy each other. Equality guarantees mutually assured destruction. Nature is violent and savage consisting of a struggle for survival/existence ending in death. There is a horrendous scale of unpleasant death in nature. Nature is permanently at war.

Savages were seen by the civilized world as drawing no distinction between violent and natural death. This savagery continues to this day within any form of martial or military culture. The Other says, "You are going to die someday anyway, and is not going to be nice, so you might as well die for your country or a good cause". The only difference here, in this example, between normality and perversion (as a form of involution) is that the normal Other only says this during times of war.

Hobbes holds that a major reason for the existence of government is to ensure that individuals are treated justly: that they are not robbed or assaulted, that their property is secure, and that their lives are regulated by rules rather than the whims of the powerful. The form of a state is its constitution, its matter is its citizens, and its purpose is to allow us to live the best life in common. In Hobbes theory, what after the French revolution came to be known as equality was occupied by a principle of Justice. Justice grants positive equality, while equality without justice yields negative equality. Negative equality is simply destructiveness, or where those who don't know, claim to know more than those who do, and where those who worked hard for what they have and their standing in society are destroyed by those who have not and not due to the lack of opportunity.

For political life the central virtue of the polis is justice, and Plato and Aristotle held different views about our motives for being just. Aristotle claims that the person who does not need political justice, or who accepts things just as they are, is either a beast or a divine being. Animals, for their part, cannot form political societies, since they lack speech and reason, while divine beings are individually self-sufficient and do not need political association. But animals can accept their fate in the same way that humans construct and accept their destiny.

At the same time, Aristotle believed that the talent for political rule is not widely distributed, and politics, therefore, is intrinsically "aristocratic". Leaders ought to be loyal to the constitution, have a great capacity to do the duties of the office, and possess virtue and a strong sense of justice. Leaders obtain and preserve their social goods due to their virtues and do not preserve their virtues due to their external material goods. Talent can recognize its presence in others, and this ensures the choice of a nonhereditary aristocracy, from then on called a modern representative government. How is this representative government if it does not concern the interest of the majority, but the interests of the few who transmit the One for the Many?

When the Many cannot reach the One, then the Many cannot be benefitted by the talent of the few or the One selected by nature to be the repository of talent to guide the Many. Without the One being able to reach the Many, the Many do not benefit from the One. However, the One is chosen by natural talent and not by aristocratic heredity or popular vote. The One, potentially, although less likely according to the size of population or limited access to a free-thinking education, can come from any socio-economic background. Representative democracy unites the common sense of the many with the talent of the few. This is a universally valid form of government. Talent and meritocracy in principle are the best form of government: the best people rule because they possess judgment, courage, justice, and moderation in the highest degree.

According to Aristotle, the three virtuous forms of government resulting from talent are kingship, aristocracy, and politeia, in which one, a few, or many persons possess ultimate power and employ it to govern for the sake of the common good. When kinship deviates from the constitution, the result is tyranny. Aristocracy can degenerate into oligarchy, and a constitutional government degenerates into democracy, where only the needs of the poor are considered. For Aristotle, neither tyranny, oligarchy, nor democracy governs with a view to the well-being of the community. The three represent different forms of special interests rather the overall good of the community.

However, before going any further we need to qualify what is meant nowadays by aristocracy because for the modern world the connection between talent and aristocracy is no longer obvious. Talent, or the One, although not widely distributed within the general population, since only 1 is required from the working class, and not only from a privileged class for which education and critical thinking may not be a priority. Aristocracy does not mean wealth or a class of hereditary nobles but simply means government by the noble in spirit and talent that can come from any social group, given facilitating circumstances, although this is not always the case.

Kingship and aristocracy, otherwise defined by class and wealth, eventually move away from talent and education and devolve into trivial forms of formalism and various forms of corruption. Formalism helps keep the monarchy and the aristocracy above the political fray, and the lack of education of the aristocracy and wealthy class prevents critical reason from questioning the cultural manners and traditions that contribute to the general civility of the population regardless of "know-how" or political orientation. In England, the Tories and the Labor Party may want to kill each other but they both must be civil before the Queen and the history of the people that she represents. This function of the alpha female has also been observed in the primate groups.

The corrupt forms of government are tyranny, in the form of oligarchy, or the tyranny of the Many or the hegemony of the working class, or a ruling monarch without a parliament or representatives of the people, and where one person, a few men, or the poor Many govern in their own narrow selfish interests. The democrats are the "poor many", and like in many societies, as a class, the poor resent the better-off and will try to seize their wealth by whatever means necessary. The Many without the One wish to secure both the benefits of aristocracy and the benefits of democracy without the defects of either.

Aristotle did not believe that the many are driven to revolt by sheer need, since following Freud and Lacan human need is never as simple as in animals. In humans, we must distinguish between need, demand, and desire. Nowadays need looks like desire, and economic demand is permeated by psychical demands rather than the simple demands of need and this helps the economy. Here we observe how current revolts in developing countries that have significantly cut their poverty rates now reflect social discontent centered around income inequality rather than poverty per se.

Social demands always exceed biological demand and represent a measure of psychical desire. To distinguish instinctual need in animals and desire in human beings, a cultural symbolic order is required. Aristotle had no sympathy with an aspiration for economic equality, precisely for this very reason. His politics is founded on the belief that nature provides for differences in intellectual and other virtues. Aristotle did not doubt that the rich were generally entitled to their wealth and social position.

In this view wealth and social position follow from meritocracy and talent. Nevertheless, and contrary to this, Aristotle's real interest is what to do if societies cannot simply rely on "the best One-man rule" because it easily degenerates into tyranny and democracy in the sense of mob rule. The problem with relying only on the One, at the expense of the Many, is that the corruption of the One is a high stakes gamble, if the Many depend on an uncorrupt One for their survival and well-being.

One of Aristotle's most famous distinctions was the one he drew between the mere gregariousness of bees and cattle and the political character of human beings. In other words, the distinction refers to the difference between biological instinct and culture and their mutual effect on species evolution. Hobbes later twisted this distinction to his own ends, claiming that Aristotle had described ants and bees as naturally political and going on to argue that humans were not naturally political precisely because they had to establish political communities by agreement on principles of justice.

Humans are not naturally political in the sense that politics is not determined by biological predispositions but by evolutions within language and the capacity for symbolic representation. The evolution of language and global communication also redefines the notion of an ideal polis since for Aristotle the ideal polis would not have more than 10,000 citizens, so that all citizens can know one another. In the computer and internet age, all citizens may know each other virtually, despite the shortcomings of a digitalized and impersonal world, but will not know each other in the sense meant by Aristotle.

Aristotle is perhaps the first author of a theory of education. A true education is devoted to knowing things that are worth knowing for their own sake and that practical reason calculates will make a young person into a man or a woman, a lady, or a gentleman, within the culture. Although the value of education, or of the One, cannot be measured or calculated in monetary value, it guarantees that knowledge associated with industry and science is used for the service of the Many. The definition of education as a gentle-person's education persisted into modern times is an indispensable element of a civilized non-violent society.

From the heights of Greek thought in Plato and Aristotle, Western society turned to the practical Roman thought of Polybius and Cicero. Regarding this historical transition, there are two views. First, the Romans took from the Greeks what they found useful but believed that Athens fell because they had too much negative equality, and they sought to prevent this from happening to the Roman Empire. However, despite the aspiration to improve upon Greek democracy, the Roman political organization failed in this task.

Thus, the Roman Empire fell by erring on the opposite side of the problem: a corrupt and unequal empire based on force rather than principle was overrun by less disciplined and more violent Barbarians. The word Barbarian simply meant foreigners who spoke "gibberish". This formulation, if warranted by historical evidence, would prove Aristotle's claim that democracy in the form of the tyranny of the Many (Greece) eventually leads to autocracy or the tyranny of the few (Rome). The fall of Athens can at least be partially attributed to negative equality and the tyranny of the Many, while Rome fell due to the tyranny of the few. This cycle can be seen repeated once again in the French revolution.

Roman thought was more practical than speculative. The Romans maximized formal and technical reason and were less proficient in the higher forms of reason, although not entirely, since eventually they found them and promoted them in the form of the Greek school of Stoicism.

In Book VI of *The Histories*, Polybius (1927) describes the political, military, and moral institutions that allowed the Romans to succeed. Polybius concludes that the Romans are the pre-eminent power because they have customs and institutions which promote a deep desire for noble acts, a love of virtue, a piety towards parents and elders, and a fear of the gods (deisidaimonia). Political power was exercised in the service of principle.

It is interesting that the Romans believed that democracy, as the rule of the Many, or egalitarianism, led tŏ negative equality or to equality as a negative factor that prevails when vertical meritocracy is not preserved. When the principles of the meritorious few or One prevails over those of the Many, then Justice emphasizes positive equality or that all people are noble and equal and have an absolute value as a human being.

Why does Nature assign talent to the One or the few? The survival of the fittest? Only the One survives? This does not seem to be the case. To prevent that the Many prevail over the One or the ideals of civilization, natural justice balances negative equality by assigning talent to the One or the few rather than making it widely distributed among the population. On the other hand, the natural talent of the One requires the support not only of the Many but also of other ancestral One's recognized as such by the Many. In a functional symbolic system, the smartest and most principled have the interests of the Many and the common good at heart.

In contrast to the Greeks and Romans, Machiavelli's *The Prince and The Discourses* (2021) mock philosophers and emphasize the teachings of practical or pragmatic experience, of real men, and yet the fact remains that Aristotle's ideal remains the rule of laws, not men.

Neither peace nor prosperity will be secure if the constitution gives workers the absolute power. On the other hand, class warfare is inevitable if a wealthy upper class monopolizes political power and exploits the lower classes. That aristocracies degenerate into oligarchies is the most common complaint against aristocratic governments and often leveled at their modern descendants, the elected aristocrats and senators who occupy the seats of power in the modern democratic world. The primary process in politics is a way of guaranteeing that aristocrats would rule the senate so the large house of representatives can be held in check by those of noble spirits. The aristocrats guarantee that wealth will be distributed according to need and talent and not simply the few rich.

The rule of talent, hard work, and meritocracy equals rule by laws and ideas and rejects oligarchy, mob rule, and despotism. This is where aristocracy and democracy meet as the best form of government. Constitutional democracy ruled by talent and the protection of minority rights, whether the minorities are the educated elite with an interest in the welfare of the Many or the vulnerable that the society must protect.

A constitutional democracy is composed of two necessary and key ingredients: public intellectuals and a prosperous middle class. When government frees intellectuals to think freely under the law, then this furthers the development of science and the virtues of thought. Here freedom of thought, which does not threaten the social order, is more important than common sense, in the sense of obedience or subordination to the rules of the social order.

Freedom of thought also requires affective and effective virtue. Temperance and equanimity are the corresponding emotional effects of practical reason and reason in its proper sense. Common sense reduces reason to only techne and formal reason but stifles or suppresses the manifestation of practical reason, Sophia, and Nous. The reduction of reason, to only two of its five forms, results in an inability of an educational system to do anything more than repeat and improve what has already been invented.

This translates into the question of social mobility: can the middle class grow into the leadership class, and can the lower marginal class grow into the middle class? This was not true in France, but the aristocracy of Britain was ready to accept into its ranks those who made money from trade. Nobility and an office could be bought in France, but the social boundaries of the English nobility were indistinct, which made being an outsider a less painful question. In contrast, the aristocracy of France was a caste. This again is a shared trait between China and the English, although I doubt that an English man would have been accepted into Chinese imperial nobility, and vice versa.

## Meritocracy

Meritocracy is a concept as old as the world itself; however, it has acquired new meaning in a contemporary society beset by problems linked to a growing gap in income inequality. According to this point of view, meritocracy is still rigged in favor of the wealthy and privileged at the expense of the most intelligent and hardest working. If only we could replace the forces of aristocracy, oligarchy, and corruption with a genuine meritocracy, then we would have a just and equal society. While others argue that meritocracy itself is the problem, it produces radical inequality, stifles social mobility, and makes everyone miserable.

Meritocracy here can be contrasted with the notion of social solidarity. From the point of view of social solidarity, people can think of meritocracy as a form of oppression since it perpetuates inequalities and privileges. What happens to those who cannot compete because of low intelligence, have concentration or emotional problems, or do everything right but then cannot find a job and this, they are told, is due to their own limitations?

The problem becomes one not of revisionism but of revisioning the meaning of excellence and merit. I argue, following many, that the excellence of merit comes from merit for its own sake or no merit, rather than from the overt and direct pursuit of profit and gaining ideas. It is not much a question of lowering our standards to good enough but rather to understand them correctly. How can meritocracy reach a broad shared prosperity among mid-skilled workers?

With respect to this point the book argues that there is a difference, not so much between polarized and compressed meritocracy but between a meritocracy based on merit and a concept of merit based on no-merit, or a concept of effort without an idea of profit or gaining, where meticulous effort is exerted for its own sake. Merit does not do anything for the person's individual ego only for the subject that is a collectivity according to Lacan. In my opinion rising inequality is not the product of meritocracy itself but of the direct search for profit and competition rather than excellence.

Under capitalism the bourgeoisie works harder at high skilled jobs than they used to and more than the working class, and they get most of their income by working. There are statistical studies that show this very clearly.

However, this analysis suffers from two errors. First, this situation does not mean that the middle class cannot improve its educational level and get high skilled jobs, although the odds are not in their favor. Second, this argument seems to imply that talent is a function of opportunity and is made. However, talent, especially superior talent, is assigned by nature, and it can come from any social class, rich or poor. An assignment from nature still needs to become a work well-done. So, the key is to educate the talented to keep the interests of the culture and the Many uppermost.

A government cannot simply be the government of the best or a meritocracy of talent without the interests of the Many or the people being involved. Otherwise, meritocracy leads to rising inequality and disrupts mechanisms of social mobility despite equal opportunities. On the other hand, a government of the people that excludes meritocracy leads to autocracy or the tyranny of the majority. The tyranny of the Many transforms into the tyranny of the One because neither term can be dialectically negated by a binary negation.

In any analysis, both terms need to be included. One must weigh the negative side effects of meritocracy against the relative risk that a government of the people could take the form of the tyranny of the Many. Of course, ideally the government of the people would include a sense of solidarity with differences of various kinds, and advocates of solidarity count on this for their arguments, but we all know, as history shows, that the origin of this structure is in the family, and that families are a source of both joy and suffering, solidarity and discordance and dissension, celebration, and drama. The conflict in the city is between brothers, and fratricidal wars are the bloodiest. Wolf is a wolf to man as in the case of Cain and Abel and Romulus and Remus.

The welfare state includes a sense of solidarity with the disabled, disadvantaged, including those who for various reasons refuse or cannot, work and nevertheless still have the rights that citizenship affords.

The criminal element within society is continuous with the market and the law as well. Here the question is whether a society tolerates those who can, but refuse to work, at the expense of those who work, or whether those who refuse are not given a choice and must accept the employment and training that the government offers them. Clearly anybody who wants to work needs to be given a job and an opportunity to advance. However, governments will fail on one side or the other. Liberal governments fail to order those who refuse to work, and socialist governments fail to recognize the need for individual freedom and the merits of "doing nothing" and how this results in something that benefits the social good.

Liberal meritocracy leaves aside those individuals who want to remain marginalized, while social meritocracy does not, but risks the dangers that come from involuntary employment and re-education that otherwise may be preferred over an indifference to the plight and security risks posed by the marginalized. In this sense, I believe the Chinese government is in the right to order to compel to work the marginalized and destructive to the most general social welfare. On the other hand, this principle has been abused.

In traditional Chinese culture, for example, the very definition of the word China in Chinese is based on the concept that the middle includes and/or pacifies/civilizes the extremes. This is conformity with the way things are (Dao) rather than mediocrity or conformism.

Both have strengths and problems because there is no complete system. Human beings need examples of both, and both should focus on improving their own shortcomings rather than the other. The problem is not that meritocracy in internally contradictory and therefore unsustainable. Meritocracy represents a true contradiction where true merit is centered around no-merit. Only a meritocracy without no-merit at its center leads to rising income inequality. And a no-merit work culture does not mean forcing people to work for free. No-merit is an intrinsic spiritual quality.

The problem with egalitarianism and equality is that they are not the same since the first can result in negative equality where the best developments are discarded by a conformist or mediocre majority. In truth we are all equal at one level and different at another. From a horizontal level we are all equal, while on a vertical level we are not. In a vertical dimension everyone is different, either one step ahead or behind everyone else, even though this may not be formally stated or recognized by external signs of hierarchical authority.

Notice that this book stays clear of giving a partisan view of politics and democracy. To choose by vote is not only an effect of the persuasiveness of political discourse, since political parties chose a candidate to persuade the public based on emotional or psychological factors, pretty much how a merchandise is sold in the marketplace.

(Fromm, 1955)

Humans are not naturally political in the sense that politics is not determined by biological predispositions but by evolutions within language and the capacity for symbolic representation. This is also related to the question of education of the individual and the group. In schools, classes are evaluated by the performance of individuals and their interactions with others. Education represents the One or the principle of excellence and non-violence used for the service of the Many. The rule of talent, hard work, and meritocracy equals rule by laws and ideas and rejects oligarchy, mob rule, and despotism. May military power, and nuclear power, rest only on those who follow a benevolent constitution, in this we trust, Oh Lord.

## References

Aristotle. (1912). *Politics: A Treatise on Government*. Mint Editions. https://bookshop. org/shop/minteditions. Accessed May 8, 2023.

Confucius (Kong Tzi). (1938). *The Wisdom of Confucius*. Edited and translated with notes by Lin Yutang. New York Random House.

Freud, S. (1913). *Totem and Taboo*. SE 13, 1–161.

Fromm, E. (1955). *The Sane Society*. New York: Fawcett Publications.

Hobbes, T. (1651). *Leviathan*. New York: Collier Books, 1962.

Machiavelli, N. (2021). *The Prince*. Oviedo: King Salomon.

Marx, K. (1872). The German Ideology. In: *The Marx-Engels Reader*, eds. Robert Tucker. New York: Norton and Company, 1972, 146–202.

Plato. (2013). *The Republic*. Book I. Cambridge, MA: Harvard University Press.

Polybius (1927). *Polybius: The Histories. The Loeb Classical Library* (in Ancient Greek, English, and Latin). Translated by Paton, W.R. London; New York: William Heinemann; G.P. Putnam's Sone.

Ryan, A. (2012). *On Politics: A History of Political Thought: From Herodotus to the Present* (2 Vol. Set). New York: Norton.

Weber, M. (1920). *The Protestant Ethic and the Spirit of Capitalism*. New York: Charles Scribners's Sons, 1958.

Wrangham, R. (2019). *The Goodness Paradox*. New York: Vintage Books.

# 6 Practice and Labor as Undivided Activity, Alienated Labor, and the Question of Surplus Value

Marx (1910) believed that the capitalist's share of the proceeds of production is unearned and represents unpaid labor. Marx also believed that at the point where the worker creates surplus value, the proletarian works for nothing, just as slaves and peasants performing unpaid labor services. This book argues that there is a difference between nothingness and emptiness. In Chan Buddhism (as well as Pauline Christianity) Pai Chang's Chan monastic rule of one day of not working is one day of not eating resolves the problem between monasticism and ordinary life, between monasticism and Protestantism, and between empty surplus production and work for nothing, the former adding to the spiritual and material prosperity of the nation. Service and work become identical forms of activity.

This is worldly or secular asceticism, whether Judeo-Christian or Buddhist, that increases both material and spiritual riches. People could chose to serve in a monastery rather than the military. However, the activity is not done for the profit, profit comes as a side effect, an added value. The rich remain motivated to work rather than simply the worker who works for subsistence only. Since talent is distributed by nature, not by society, or popular vote, the division of labor based on education and skill is not intrinsically unfair or unjust. Unfairness only occurs, when the less educated do not have access to education.

The tradition of the Freudian Left understood work as a form of alienated anal-retentive compulsion. The cultural sexual morality which Freud was seen as making responsible for the massive creation of neurosis was considered, therefore, the historical twin of a developing capitalist Protestant "work morality". The more the guilt is associated with waste and leisure, the more the compulsive subject will want to work. In the sixteenth and seventeenth centuries, prior to protestant work morality, people worked long enough to earn as much needed to subsist.

While the bourgeoisie, with the development of the capitalist work morality, no longer sees creative productivity beyond mere subsistence as alienated labor, when this work morality is imposed on wage laborers, supposedly for their own good, it creates the conditions for alienated labor under colonialism and capitalism. To both escape alienation and increase profits at the same

DOI: 10.4324/9781003403012-7

time, the worker must become a consumer like the capitalist. In addition, and for example, this partly explains the difference in development between North America and South America. Despite slavery in North America, the colonizers also worked under a work ethic, and this was not simply imposed on the workers while the bosses idly sat by watching them work.

We know since the time of Lao Tzi and Kong Zi and then with Locke (1704) and Cromwell in England that a situation where "Many labor under conditions of alienated labor for a One that no longer works" is not good for a commonwealth or common prosperity. A commonwealth, and its governance, must balance the talents and riches of the One with the needs of the Many. Nevertheless, there remains a gap between ideals and how the same ideals may result in practical mistreatment regardless of political orientation. A commonwealth is a principled way to speak about social capitalism, since capitalism by itself speaks of a system and a culture centered around profit, not much better than mercantilism. This situation differs from ideology that puts a nice face on to rapacious relations of domination. Critical reason is a critique of relations of domination.

Marx believed that at the point where the worker creates surplus value, the proletarian works for nothing, just as slaves and peasants performing unpaid labor services. However, Marx did not understand the meaning of nothing or the difference between nothingness and emptiness. In Chan Buddhism (as well as Pauline Christianity) Pai Chang's Chan monastic rule of one day of not working is one day of not eating and resolves the problem between monasticism and ordinary life, between monasticism and Protestantism, between empty surplus production and work for nothing, and the spiritual and material prosperity of the nation. In the history of China, work practice as a form of Chan practice prevented the persecution of Chan in China and allowed the transmission to eventually flow from China to Japan and Korea in the form of Zen.

An evolved society in the future will base surplus capital and production on emptiness, as an inexhaustible source of energy, whether this be solar fusion or a direct access to the power of emptiness itself. Currently the worker does not work for nothing. Rather the worker works for Emptiness (Kong) in the process of joining the middle class in one or two generations. They work to pay for their new standard of life in cities with or without a social safety net.

Ordinary employers driven by rational instrumental self-interest will want workers to work as long as possible for as little as possible, and employees driven by the same motivation will want to be paid as much as possible for as little work as possible and each side would like the legal system to favor its interests.

The tradition of Freudian-Marxism understood work labor as a form of alienated anal-retentive compulsion. The cultural sexual morality which Freud made responsible for the massive creation of neurosis is, therefore, the historical twin of a developing capitalist Protestant "work morality". The more the guilt is associated with waste and leisure, the more the compulsive subject will want to work. In the sixteenth and seventeenth centuries, prior to protestant work morality, people worked long enough to earn as much needed to subsist.

While the bourgeoisie, with the development of the capitalist work morality, no longer sees creative productivity beyond mere subsistence as alienated labor, when this work morality is imposed on wage laborers, supposedly for their own good, it created the conditions for alienated labor under capitalism. Before capitalism, the assumption was that non-alienated labor is limited to earn as much money needed to subsist. Then Marx considers the opposite: under capitalism the worker is alienated because they are limited to subsistence wages while the capitalist extracts the surplus value of their labor. However, as already stated, prior to the protestant ethics, there was no compulsion to work beyond what was necessary to survive.

If the worker under capitalism is getting survival wages for a fixed number of hours, then prior to the protestant ethics this would not be seen as alienated labor. It only becomes so when an entrepreneur or capitalist does not limit their hours or labor to pay their bills but rather their surplus labor leads to an increase of wealth and productivity. Now a CEO may be working themselves and drinking themselves to death, but they are their own boss. Within reason, and depending on the task, long work hours are not necessarily harmful to mental and physical heath.

Self-discipline, necessary repression, and work productivity are misinterpreted as oppression by its very definition, and not on the basis of specific oppressive and inhuman industrial working conditions. Symbolic structure is confused and reduced to the social control of the bourgeoisie. Symbolic castration is explained by the castrating characteristic of wage labor. A capacity for personal life, and personal life as a capacity, does not belong to the worker anymore, as if there could not be enjoyment for the worker in many menial or hard forms of labor.

Of course, with the growth of the middle class, or the bourgeoisie as the largest social group, including blue collar or industrial workers, the personal life of the worker is now spent in entertainment and the consumption of many optional (some would say questionable) forms of comfort that also fuel the economy. What was interpreted as a form of social castration under a labor regime without any enjoyment, becomes the enjoyment of the surplus generated by labor, and rising wages leading to demand and consumption.

At the same time, it is impossible not to bring the question of the division of labor to bear on the nature of work, for the simple reason, that harsh and degrading forms of physical labor are not only difficult on the body but also on the mind. However, when the mind is trained through education and spiritual practice, not only does the human mind lead to mental forms of labor that are less physically exhausting, but physical labor itself becomes bearable when practiced with the right spirit.

For example, digging ditches, moving rocks, gardening, cooking, carpentry, cleaning floors and windows, in a Chan monastery, all become universal forms of enlightened activity. The body may be tired, but the spirit is clear and clarified by physical labor. A similar point was made by St Paul: "He who will not work shall not eat". Work is a form of grace. People need to work even if wealthy, not to support their needs but to be redeemed by the grace that comes from work. This is worldly asceticism, whether Christian or Buddhist.

John Wesley (1738), on the other hand, argued that when riches increase, religion decreases. In other words, when labor done for its own sake leads to riches, then the profit motive supersedes the drive to work based on grace or enlightened human activity. As riches increase, pride, anger, and the wishes of the flesh also increase. For Wesley only the poor remain obedient and had a true and pure motivation for work. From this perspective, surplus productivity translated into the financial gain of the few eventually becomes the end of true surplus production.

Since talent is distributed by nature, not by society, or popular vote, the division of labor on the basis of education and skill is not intrinsically unfair or unjust. Unfairness only occurs, when the less educated do not have access to education. If the less educated and talented do not seek education, not because of social obstacles or impediments but because of a deficit of motivation or desire, or personal problems, then the division of labor in this case is not systematically exploitative. This formulation helps organize prior thinking on the division of labor that was dual or ambivalent: some saw it as intrinsically destructive, and some saw it as inevitable and necessary. In the end, the division of labor is both constructive and destructive.

Income inequality was already a concern during Cromwell times. In 1650, Cromwell wrote to the Long Parliament: "Be pleased to reform the abuses of all professions: and if there be anyone that makes many poor to make a few rich, that suits not a commonwealth". A commonwealth, and its governance, has to balance the talents and needs of the One with the talents and needs of the Many. Only when the Many accept the One, then can the Many effectively become One. When the One rejects the Many, then the Many cannot access the One. When the Many reject the One of nature and natural talent, then the Many will fail to accede to the One of virtue and excellence.

The key question in any society is where resources beyond those required for subsistence are generated and how such capital resources benefit the One or the Many.

Marx counts technological imagination and scientific discovery as forces of production, but he first sees the state as the instrument of the ruling class, which is the dominant economic class, and the state manages its common interests. However, far from suffering "immiseration", the English working-man had half a century of rising real wages. This was destructive of Marx's hopes of revolution.

England, and the industrial revolution, gave refuge to Marx as the intellectual leader of a social revolution with laudable human aspirations and at the same contained and surpassed the limitations of the revolutionary Marxist project. Market economies, for example, have created a huge middle class more concerned with their living standards than any revolutionary ideology. Nations here can appeal to their own talent and to the best of their cultural traditions without compromising the values of either socialism or a free market economy.

By the same token, if government officials see the positions they occupy as positions of service, not authority, then presumably they would feel no desire to exploit their authority. Corruption is a danger to any large bureaucracy or corporation, especially when power and money are involved.

Hobbes's (1651) analysis of the state of nature, the war of all against all, is a frighteningly apt rendering of a world where nuclear powers faced each other with the power to destroy the earth. In addition, internationalism and egalitarianism turned out to be less attractive than nationalism for countries and less attractive than individual economic advancement for the individual. Nonetheless, a much-diluted semi-socialism has been the salvation of capitalism. A European social-democratic welfare state with a liberal and private market economy is still to be set up in socialist countries under a capitalist economic system. The twentieth century was a century of revolution, but its revolutions were all too often the prelude to dictatorial and totalitarian regimes.

The aristocratic critique of modern society runs thus: in a healthy society, the cultural – and therefore the political – tone is set by an elite whose title to act as an elite stem from tradition and a consensus that they know what excellence is. In contrast to the United States, those in the nonelite are not cut off from the elite, but they defer to the elite's leadership and expect to be educated into its standards. An unhealthy society has substituted mass tastes and inclinations, which are instinctually motivated, for cultural values of a different nature that are required for the constructive manifestation of instinct within human beings.

The United States is a nation of loudmouths, not of shrinking violets. But the loudmouths in a litigious society make planning beyond an election cycle impossible. This is why many say California, as a state, has become unmanageable. Instead of a federal state of 400 million, imagine 1 billion loudmouths in a large territory (like China) that could make management and distribution impossible. China quietly and humbly succeeded where other did not, because quietly, without searching profit, accomplished and amazing task. Solar panels in Europe or the US were very expensive and were outselling the lower quality Chinese product. The Chinese government made a forty year plan that their solar panels would be cheaper and better than the American and European panels and at a lower price. Only a one party system could accomplish this.

The loudmouths are also linked to a free press and to public opinion shaped by a free press. However, a free press may not be free and simply be a space for blaming and bullying or stereotypical prejudicial speech. This is what people call fake news. The news emotionally describe personal tragedies and focus on the palace intrigue and sexual escapades of the rich and famous.

On the other hand, an official and censored state-sponsored press only, cannot qualify as freedom of thought or a free press. True freedom of thought and a free press lie somewhere between these two positions. Here the standard would have to be an independent and non-political newscast respected by the majority and that is able to objectively examine the merits of various points of view and not only those of a dominant and repressive state.

The role of a free press is to openly discuss the conceptual alternatives and choices facing the national interest without the pressure of partial and contentious political interests leading to unintended historical and political consequences and civil disorder. Decisions must be made by leaders with big hearts and calm analytical skills, such as those exemplified by the women leaders of the six nations that were most successful in containing the pandemic of Covid 19.

The creature who expresses her or his opinions on the airwaves is not thinking, but parroting, the equivalent of idle speech in psychoanalysis. "Public opinion", to which politicians supposedly defer, but spend their time manipulating, is a loud noise made by a flock of birds flying in a circle inside one's head, not the speech of citizens. Freedom of the press does not guarantee the quality of a civilization, unless the One can also manifest within the culture.

The five forms of reason, or the One, can be suppressed by censorship or by the flat two-dimensionality of the culture. Free press, freedom of thought, and academic freedom are intrinsically linked. Free press without freedom of scientific or rational thought degenerates into mob rule and the dictatorship of the uneducated Many, and freedom of thought without a free press leads to aristocracy in the sense of despotism or oligarchy. Without freedom of thought or a free press, a civilization decays not into mob rule but into a dictatorship of the Many, however rule-bound the Many may be. Talent and discovery suffer in this case. The culture may fabricate or manufacture goods but may not accede to the higher level of creativity needed for theory and the invention of the new. This could be true of China or America. A "Martinette" "Tin pot" dictator pretends to represent the people but is a weak cruel dictator hindering their growth.

## References

Hobbes, T. (1651). *Leviathan*. New York: Collier Books, 1962.

Locke, J. (1704). *Political Writings. Cambridge Texts in the History of Political Thought*. Ed. Mark Goldie. Cambridge: CUP, 2002.

Marx, K. (1910). *Theories of Surplus Value*. London: Lawrence and Wishart, 1951.

Wesley, J. (1738). *The Complete Sermons*. Oxford: Hargreaves Publishing.

# 7 The One and the Many

In this chapter, I will excavate the intellectual roots of the One and the Many concepts and differentiate them from its near enemies, and how they can be misinterpreted, especially within political theory and the ordinary doxa or political opinion with which people live. The concepts come from Heraclitus and Parmenides, Buddha (Avatamsaka Sutra, and Huayan in China), Plotinus, and Lacan. The terms are featured in the motto of the United States "E plu·ri·bus U·num", from Many, One; but from One, also Many but people not royalty.

With Plotinus (CE 204–70) and Lacan, this book argues that the One mind can only be identical to the ordinary world of common sense and the Many, based on the One's own non-being or the lack of inherent nature (the Buddhist no-self). The One's own non-being goes beyond ontology and anti-ontology, philosophy, and anti-philosophy.

Within the first turning of the wheel of the teaching, the Theravada school of Buddhism has the ascetic ideal of the Arahat who leaves the world to attain a personal enlightenment. The bodhisattva (enlightening being) instead is a Buddha-to-be or the compassionate aspect of the Buddha that renounces his/her own personal Nirvana to stay in the world and help beings realize enlightenment. Here the One has moved towards the Many rather than away from them. Just like there are many Buddhas, there are several great bodhisattvas, each with a thousand helpful arms. Every individual is the Buddha-nature and whether talented or not, rich, or poor still has the long-term potential to become Buddha (across three lifetimes).

Lacan thinks of the Buddha as constituted within a dialectic of the One and the Many. Like the monad, one yet not isolated, the Buddha is a real One and at the same time there are many Ones. This dialectic between the One and the Many is also reflected in the relationship between Buddhas and bodhisattvas. The relationship between Buddhas and bodhisattvas cannot be exactly described as hierarchical since it is outside the imaginary self-other duality. Bodhisattvas are Buddhas-to-be, and Buddhas can manifest as bodhisattvas. It is not a question of status, but one of mutual respect between beings, between teacher and student, Buddhas and bodhisattvas, analysts and analysands. In this respect, Lacan provides a fresh and unique perspective.

DOI: 10.4324/9781003403012-8

The blank slate or empty screen I redefine as one of the elements of the psyche or Mind that is shared with natural phenomena. Culture is built in the back systems of the Mind that are never saturated thanks to the empty slate/ state. In fact, the empty slate I redefine as a One empty mirror. Kindness and love are also part of the mirror of nature that is shared by animals and humans, but in humans, kindness also functions as a necessary superstructure that becomes divorced from the drive and from the natural kindness of the drive. This is an unnecessary loss and deficit, rather than a gain as Kant and German culture believed. Ethics as duty instead of the kindness of the heart can become its opposite or cruelty, while natural kindness is unmixed with its opposite for the most part. Cruelty is prevented by retaining the link between the two forms of kindness: natural and socialized or compelled, something that Confucius knew quite well. In many cases, when the link is not retained the result is some form of psychopathy or sociopathy that in leaders proves to be destructive of the social order. Justice is a calm not a violent mighty spirit. The still small voice is not heard in the streets. It handles all things carefully without harm. The cool fire of justice is kept alive without fail until it is established upon the minds of the people. "He who restrains his words has knowledge, he who has a cool spirit is a man of understanding" (Proverbs 17:27).

I argue that the relation between the One and the Many that follows from Heraclitus and Asian or Buddhist thought needs to be redefined. This involves the definition of the individual. The self-interest of the liberal individual is not the One, given that greed or selfishness does not transform into altruism or something that benefits the common good. The reason that the good of the individual and of the group can coincide is that the interests of the One include self and other, and the interests of the Many, and the interest of the Many includes the interest of each One. The Many without the One is not the true Many. The egotistical One or master of the master's discourse fits well with how Freud described leaders sometimes not as having self-mastery, but mastery in the sense of narcissism, self-confidence, and independence.

This is where Adam Smith (1759) got it both right and wrong. Right because when Many are linked to the One, the Many are benefitted by the One, but when the One is not the true One (the One's own non-being), but is rather the imaginary ego of individual self-interest, then the alleged One does not lead to the benefit of the Many. A key here is how to define self-interest whether as greed and selfishness or as creative effort in the service of a personal interest that benefits self and other alike. I argue the latter.

This question is also related to the question of the part and the whole, the individual and the State, and their mutual interdependence. The problem with the continental Hegelian and Marxist concept of the State is that it defines the individual entirely within the concept of a signifier/number or a symbolic subject that is conditioned and determined by the State as a whole. A self-enclosed system generates its own subjects/numbers.

What is missing here is the concept of the subject all alone or the One which is where three forms of nature meet and interact: animal nature or instinct; human nature, or cultural law; and Buddha nature, or the wisdom and compassion that emerge from the default nature of the void and its energy. The subject in and of the Real or the real Ego is the subject of jouissance that is outside the signifier and yet inside the Borromean knot. The subject is both a signifier and a collectivity and a Real "subject-all-Alone" within experience and yet outside language.

Here this book differs from what has been identified with Lacanian left (Laclau and Mouffe, 1985; Glynos and Stavrakakis, 2008) that only considers the subject of the signifier (as a collectivity) while ignoring Lacan's later Real ego that I call the subject of jouissance in and of the Real. The subject of jouissance, within the Borromean knot, is not irrelevant for the signifier since it provides the glue that binds the symbolic order together. Such jouissance is of a different kind in the binding of animal instinct, the binding of the ego and the master's discourse, and the letter jouissance of symbols as pure empty forms.

The subject of the signifier cannot be confused with dispersion, and metonymical displacements within language because it would ignore what Lacan said about the subject as metaphor in relationship to the Name of the Father (NoF). What provides cohesion to subjective experience and language is not the quiescence of the autonomous ego, but internal psychical and linguistic structure organized by the NoF as a function and the subject as metaphor. True subject is no subject because the subject is a metaphor. This is not a contradiction or is an example of a true contradiction.

The imaginary autonomous ego of the individual and secondary narcissism is not asocial and is symbolically and socially structured. The subject of the signifier is a collective, while the subject of the Real is neither the ego nor the signifier for it is outside the signifier and the collective structure, while at the same time not being the imaginary ego of individualism. The individual does not only represent nature but also the "citi-zen" and the subject of the laws of culture. But an individual is more than a number or a name assigned by the culture. In each beating heart resides experiences of the oneness of the One and the Many, including with animals. The Real as the void is always within signification but there are three levels of signification in Lacan: imaginary meaning, symbolic signification, and Real significance otherwise known as the Third jouissance of meaning.

The subject of the Real or jouissance is represented by the empty mirror, screen, or membrane (mem-brain). The subject can change the social structure because the subject in the Real remains unconditioned and unsaturated. This is not a revolutionary social agent, but rather the place of the lack in the system or order itself that the One embodies, as the One's own non-being. Now the All or whole includes a hole or the vacuum state generator of both the One and the Many with different polarities.

# References

Avatamsaka Sutra. (1993). Translated by Thomas Cleary. Boston, MA: Shambhala.

Glynos, J. and Stavrakakis, Y. (2008). Lacan and Political Subjectivity: Fantasy and Enjoyment in Psychoanalysis and Political Theory. *Subjectivity* 24, 256–274.

Laclau, E. and Mouffe, C. (1985). *Hegemony and Socialist Strategy: Towards a Radical Democratic Politics.* London: Verso.

Plotinus (204–70 CE [1991]). *The Enneads (Classics).* London: Penguin Books. Kindle Edition.

Smith, A. (1776). *The Wealth of Nations.* New York: A Banthan Book.

# 8 Equality, Inequality, Meritocracy, Excellence, Talent, Defect, and Disability

The question of labor under bourgeois capitalism translates into the question of social mobility: can the middle class grow into the leadership class, and can the lower marginal class grow into the middle class? This was not true in France, but the aristocracy of Britain was ready to accept into its ranks those who made money from trade. Nobility and an office could be bought in France, but the flexible social boundaries of the English nobility made being an outsider a less painful. In contrast, the aristocracy of France was a rigid caste.

Marx believed the capitalist's share of the proceeds of production is unearned and it is deducted from the total and represents unpaid labor. Marx believed that at the point where the worker creates surplus value, the proletarian works for nothing, just as slaves and peasants performing unpaid labor services do. "The labor of a menial servant, on the contrary, adds to the value of nothing... Only labor which produces capital is productive labor" (Marx, 1867, p.152). Labor is exchanged with capital because labor produces a surplus value. "The labor of some of the most respectable orders in the society is, like that of menial servants, unproductive of any value, and does not fix or realize itself in any permanent subject, or vendible commodity ..." (Smith, Book II, Chapter III, pp.294–295).

Marx considers this unproductive labor even though a subject may experience it as productive and enjoyable, as a personal service. Although a service has its labor time, it does not directly generate a commodity. I say directly because a service may help others generate an exchangeable commodity, as well as capital. However, from the point of view of capital, such services may be "incidental operating expenses", as it is called in economics, incurred in the productive investment of capital, which do not themselves add new value to output and therefore should be kept at a minimum. A writer, in this model, only becomes a productive worker from the point of view of capital when they can generate capital for their publisher. A writer agrees to this since the publisher offers to publish the book at their expense.

However, Marx did not understand a different meaning of nothing or the difference between Western nothingness and Eastern emptiness. In Chan

DOI: 10.4324/9781003403012-9

Buddhism (as well as Pauline Christianity) Pai Chang's Chan monastic rule of one day of not working is one day of not eating and resolves the problem between monasticism and ordinary life, between monasticism and Protestantism, between empty surplus production and work for nothing, and the spiritual and material prosperity of the nation. In the history of China, work practice as a form of Chan practice prevented the persecution of Chan in China and allowed the transmission to eventually flow from China to Japan and Korea in the form of Zen.

The tradition of Freudian-Marxism understood work labor as a form of alienated anal-retentive compulsion. The cultural sexual morality which Freud made responsible for the massive creation of neurosis is, therefore, the historical twin of a developing capitalist Protestant "work morality". The more the guilt is associated with waste and leisure, the more the compulsive subject will want to work. In the sixteenth and seventeenth centuries, prior to protestant work morality, people worked long enough to earn as much needed to subsist.

Ordinary employers driven by rational instrumental self-interest will want workers to work for as little as possible, and employees driven by the same motivation will want to be paid as much as possible for as little work as possible and each side would like the legal system to favor its interests.

While the bourgeoisie, with the development of the capitalist work morality, no longer sees creative productivity beyond mere subsistence as alienated labor, when this work morality is imposed on wage laborers, supposedly for their own good, it created the conditions for alienated labor under capitalism. Before capitalism, the assumption was that non-alienated labor is limited to earn as much money needed to subsist. Then Marx considers the opposite: under capitalism the worker is alienated because they are limited to subsistence wages, while the capitalist extracts the surplus value of their labor. However, as already stated, prior to the protestant ethic, there was no compulsion to work beyond what was necessary to survive.

So, if the worker under capitalism is getting survival wages for a fixed number of hours, then prior to the protestant ethic this would not be seen as alienated labor. It only becomes so when an entrepreneur or capitalist does not limit their hours or labor to pay their bills, but rather their surplus labor leads to an increase of wealth and productivity. Within reason, and depending on the task, long work hours are not necessarily harmful to mental and physical heath although they could be beyond a certain point in which the worker and the animal need food and drink.

Self-discipline, necessary repression, and work productivity are misinterpreted as oppression by its very definition, and not based on specific oppressive and/or inhuman industrial working conditions. Symbolic structure is confused and reduced to the social control of the bourgeoisie. Symbolic castration is explained by the castrating characteristic of wage labor. A capacity for personal life, and personal life as a capacity, does not belong to the worker anymore, as if there could not be enjoyment for the worker in many menial or physical forms of labor.

Of course, with the growth of the middle class, or the bourgeoisie as the largest social group, including blue collar or industrial workers, the personal life of the worker is now spent in entertainment and the consumption of many optional (some would say questionable) forms of comfort that also fuel the economy. What was interpreted as a form of social castration under a labor regime without any enjoyment, becomes the enjoyment of the surplus generated by labor, and rising wages leading to demand and consumption.

At the same time, it is impossible not to bring the question of the division of labor to bear on the nature of work, for the simple reason, that harsh and degrading forms of physical labor are not only difficult on the body but also on the mind. However, when the mind is trained through education and spiritual practice, not only does the human mind led to mental forms of labor that are less physically exhausting, but physical labor itself becomes bearable when practiced with the right spirit. For example, digging ditches, moving rocks, gardening, cooking, carpentry, cleaning floors and windows, in a Chan monastery, all become universal forms of enlightened activity. The body may be tired, but the spirit is clear and clarified by physical labor. A similar point was made by St Paul: Work is a form of grace. People need to work even if wealthy, not to support their needs but to be redeemed by the grace that comes from work. This is worldly asceticism, whether Christian or Buddhist.

Income inequality was already a concern during Cromwell times. In 1650, Cromwell wrote to the Long Parliament: "Be pleased to reform the abuses of all professions: and if there be anyone that makes many poor to make a few rich, that suits not a commonwealth". A commonwealth, and its governance, must balance the talents and needs of the One with the talents and needs of the Many. Only when the Many accept the One, then can the Many effectively become One. When the One rejects the Many, then the Many cannot access the One. When the Many reject the One of nature and natural talent, then the Many will fail to accede to the One of virtue and excellence.

The key question in any society is where resources beyond those required for subsistence are generated and how such capital resources benefit the One or the Many.

Marx counts technological imagination and scientific discovery as forces of production, but he first sees the state as the instrument of the ruling class, which is the dominant economic class, and the state manages its common interests. However, far from suffering "immiseration", the English working person had half a century of rising real wages. This was destructive of Marx's hopes of revolution in England.

England, and the industrial revolution, gave both refuge to Marx as the intellectual leader of a social revolution with laudable human aspirations, and at the same contained and surpassed the limitations of the revolutionary Marxist project. Market economies, for example, have created a huge middle class more concerned with their living standards than any revolutionary ideology. Nations here can appeal to their own talent and to the best of their cultural traditions without compromising the values of either socialism or a free market economy.

By the same token, if government officials see the positions they occupy as positions of service, not authority, then presumably they would feel no desire to exploit their authority. Corruption is a danger to any large public bureaucracy or private corporation, especially when power and money are involved.

Justice and constitution must also protect the interests of talented individuals assigned by nature. Talent may come from any class, and not only from the wealthy. Talent represents the interests of the individual that are geared towards the common collective good and therefore should be supported rather than rejected. Justice equally prevents that equality degenerate into negative equality or egalitarianism and that talent degenerate into individualistic activities that do not benefit the Many.

Intellectual and spiritual leaders, however, must choose their own spiritual successors (only talent can recognize talent in others) before leaders become confirmed by either vote or service to the people. Here we need to distinguish between political leaders and spiritual and intellectual leaders. As is often the case, the latter may help the former but do not hold political power or office. In political office, it is not only up to the leader to choose a successor. In intellectual or spiritual leadership, a leader organically chooses his or her successor based on the talent and chance factors assigned by nature. Successors, of course, must also prove themselves in relationship to the collectivity and the Other of society.

Representative democracy unites the common sense of the Many with the talent of the One. This is a universally valid form of government. Talent and meritocracy in principle are the best form of government: the best people rule in the service of the people because they possess judgment, courage, justice, and moderation in the highest degree. A democracy can also be measured by the question of social mobility.

In the cases that the working class becomes the ruling class, then the officers of the government become the middle class, and the people become either a rich upper class or a prosperous middle class. Meritocracy is a concept as old as the world itself; however, it has acquired new meaning in a contemporary society beset by problems linked to a growing gap in income inequality. According to this point of view, meritocracy is still rigged in favor of the wealthy and privileged at the expense of the most intelligent and hardest working. If only we could replace the forces of aristocracy, oligarchy, and corruption with a genuine meritocracy, then we would have a just and equal society.

Others instead argue that meritocracy itself is the problem: it produces radical inequality, stifles social mobility, and makes everyone miserable. "Personal ability is a double-edged weapon; using it may fulfill something in the individual's nature but at the cost of cutting ties to the world in which he or she has a place" (Sennett, 2011, p.28). Meritocracy here has been contrasted with the notion of social solidarity. From the point of view of social solidarity, people can think of meritocracy as a form of oppression since it perpetuates inequalities and privileges. What happens to those who cannot compete because of low intelligence, have concentration or emotional problems, or do everything right but then cannot find a job and this, they are told, is due to their own limitations?

The problem becomes one not of revisionism but of revisioning the meaning of excellence and merit. I argue that the excellence of merit comes from merit for its own sake or no merit, rather than from the overt and direct pursuit of profit and gaining ideas. It is not much a question of lowering our standards to good enough but rather to understand them correctly. How can meritocracy reach a broad shared prosperity among mid-skilled workers?

> With respect to this point the book argues that there is a difference, not so much between polarized and common meritocracy but between a meritocracy based on merit, and a concept of merit based on no-merit, or a concept of effort without an idea of profit or gaining, where meticulous effort is exerted for its own sake. "Against the seduction of envy, Rousseau argued for the virtue of amour de soi, of craft, of the self-respect which consists in doing something well for its own sake".
>
> (Sennett, 2011, p.93)

Merit does not do anything for the person's individual ego only for the subject that is a collectivity according to Lacan. In my opinion rising inequality is not the product of meritocracy itself but of the direct search for profit and competition rather than the essence of surplus value and jouissance value that leads to surplus productivity. Competition here means each one or many pursuing their personal interests in offering a similar product or service. It could be a doctor or a temple.

Economic thinking lumps together productive value and exchange value. "From surplus value in its general form we come straight to a common rate of profit, which has nothing directly to do with it" (Marx, p.131). In addition, according to Marx, Smith confuses surplus value with profit. So, we have four terms: (1) Productive value; (2) Exchange value; (3) Surplus value; and (4) Profit. I submit that the essence of surplus value is not profit, otherwise the worker becomes a commodity or transaction.

Capitalists also come in two forms: the crony kind that objectifies workers, and the ethical kind that wants to make a good product for humanity. Capital by itself is primarily interested in making a profit. If the capitalist pays good wages at first to their workers, even in the absence of revenue, then the capitalists may not expect to see profits for some time. The capitalist knows this and bets on it, and thus, the capitalist runs a risk that the worker receiving good wages does not. The worker is motivated to keep working so that company succeeds even more so if they are promised a stake in the company in the form of stocks.

A capitalist can produce for the sake of surplus value in two forms: the desire for profits, or the surplus value and jouissance raised by their cognitive interests. Here surplus jouissance is a different concept. It is a form of surplus value that is not profit. It refers to the enjoyment of productive activity as a service, as an end in itself that consumes itself in the process, and regardless of whether it produces capital, wages, or services. The crony capitalist only cares about the relative value of profit, the ethical capitalist cares about the absolute value of surplus jouissance, and the surplus value of the product or service itself and that of the enjoyment of the worker in production. Ethical capitalism invests in products that are socially responsible.

If the cognitive interest of the capitalist refers, not to profit or capital but to socially responsible investment, then there could be legitimate profit as an added value for the capitalist, resulting from the surplus productivity and surplus jouissance of the worker. This way profit is not directly related to surplus value, jouissance, or productivity and becomes an added value.

Under capitalism the bourgeoisie works harder at high skilled jobs than they used to and more than the working class, and they get most of their income by working. There are statistical studies that show this very clearly. However, this analysis suffers from two errors. First, this situation does not mean that the middle class cannot improve its educational level and get high skilled jobs, although the odds are not in their favor. Second, this argument seems to imply that talent is a function of opportunity and is made. However, talent, especially superior talent, is assigned by nature, and it can come from any social class, rich or poor. An assignment from nature still needs to become a work well-done. So, the key is to educate the talented to keep the interests of the culture and the Many uppermost.

A government cannot simply be the government of the best or a meritocracy of talent without the interests of the Many or the people being involved. Otherwise, meritocracy leads to rising inequality and disrupts mechanisms of social mobility despite equal opportunities. On the other hand, a government of the people that excludes meritocracy leads to autocracy or the tyranny of the majority. The tyranny of the Many transforms into the tyranny of the One because neither term can be dialectically negated by a binary negation. In any analysis, both terms need to be included.

One must weigh the negative side effects of meritocracy against the relative risk that a government of the people could take the form of the tyranny of the Many. Of course, ideally the government of the people would include a sense of solidarity with differences of various kinds, and advocates of solidarity count on this for their arguments, but we all know, as history shows, that the origin of this structure is in the family and that families are a source of both joy and suffering, solidarity and discordance and dissension, celebration, and drama. The conflict in the city is between brothers, and fratricidal wars are the bloodiest. Wolf is a wolf to man as in the case of Cain and Abel and Romulus and Remus.

The welfare state includes a sense of solidarity with the disabled, disadvantaged, including those who for various reasons refuse or cannot, work and nevertheless still have the rights that citizenship affords. "For the low-IQ masses, meritocracy proves personally unbearable to them".

(Sennett, 2011, p.27)

The criminal element within society is continuous with the market and the law as well. Here the question is whether a society tolerates those who can but refuse to work at the expense of those who work, or whether those who refuse are not given a choice and must accept the employment and training that the government offers them. Clearly anybody who wants to work needs to be given a job and an opportunity to advance. However, governments will fail on one side or the other.

Liberal meritocracy leaves behind those individuals who want to remain marginalized, while social meritocracy does not, but risks the dangers that come from involuntary employment and re-education that otherwise may be preferred over an indifference to the plight and security risks posed by the marginalized. In traditional Chinese culture, for example, the very definition of the word China in Chinese is based on the concept that the middle includes and/or pacifies/civilizes the extremes outside the center. This is conformity with the way things are (Dao) rather than mediocrity or conformism.

Both have strengths and problems because there is no complete system. Human beings need examples of both, and both should focus on improving their own shortcomings rather than the other. The problem is not that meritocracy is internally contradictory and therefore unsustainable. Meritocracy represents a true contradiction where true merit is centered around no-merit. Only a meritocracy without no-merit at its center leads to rising income equality.

The problem with egalitarianism and equality is that they are not the same since the first can result in negative equality where the best developments are discarded by a conformist or mediocre majority. In truth, we are all equal at one level and different at another. From a horizontal level we are all equal, while on a vertical level we are not. In a vertical dimension everyone is different, always either one step ahead or behind everyone else, even though this may not be formally stated or recognized by external signs of hierarchical authority.

Notice that this book stays clear of giving a partisan view of politics and democracy. To choose by vote is not only an effect of the persuasiveness of political discourse, since political parties chose a candidate to persuade the public based on emotional or psychological factors, pretty much how a merchandise is sold in the marketplace (Fromm, 1955).

Humans are not naturally political in the sense that politics is not determined by biological predispositions but by evolutions within language and the capacity for symbolic representation. This is also related to the question of education of the individual and the group. In schools, classes are evaluated by the performance of individuals and their interactions with others. Education represents the One or the principle of excellence and non-violence used for the service of the Many. The rule of talent, hard work, and meritocracy equals rule by laws and ideas and rejects oligarchy, mob rule, and despotism.

# References

Fromm, E. (1955). *The Sane Society*. New York: Fawcett Publications.
Marx, K. (1867). Theories of Surplus Value, Volume IV of Capital part two. London: Lawrence and Wishart, 1969.
Sennett, R. (2011). *Respect in a World of Inequality*. New York: Norton.

# 9 Animal and Human Spirits or Jouissance in the Economy

John Maynard Keynes (1935) coined the term "animal spirits" to refer to emotional mindsets. Emotions have a strong presence in economic decision-making. Keynes wrote that investment decisions "can only be taken as a result of animal spirits".

According to this point of view, confidence or lack of it can drive or hamper economic growth. But as we have seen, confidence is also a confidence in the principles of the human spirit. The value of the good life is more satisfying than the pleasure afforded by material goods although the two work together.

For Keynes, economic decisions are intuitive, emotional, and irrational. But expectations or illusions of profit or success surprisingly are not the only animal factor affecting confidence.

The function of culture is to teach subjects how to succeed despite not without failure. This is the good life worth living for. I think it was Becket who said: "Ever try, ever fail, occasionally succeed, fail better" and feel better. Loss is necessary for success. Fairness is linked to the function of culture of regulating the drives and the animal spirits resulting in some form of self-discipline.

Culture or C = Phi or Phi = Phi. Phi = 1.618. Culture or C = is defined by the subtraction of the object of the drive from the subject, and this has the numerical value 1. When the function, definition, or concept of Culture that has the numerical value of 1.618 subtracts the object of desire and the drive from the subject (numerical value 0.618), the result is an imaginary enchanted number (1) as a measure of jouissance value in symbolic exchange and a ratio of desire. The loss (of the object) of jouissance shows the equivalence between the culture and the function of symbolic castration, as being the same or identical. Symbolic castration is also an indication of jouissance.

The normal psychical losses of the subject in the family and their elaborations prepare the subject to procure the gains and sustain the losses afforded by social goods and objects of consumption. This I argue is what Keynes referred to as animal spirits in the marketplace.

The use value or the labor value of the object is not its jouissance value that cannot be measured in rational numbers. Jouissance value is measured

DOI: 10.4324/9781003403012-10

in irrational and complex numbers, this is one of my hypotheses. A complex number carries both, the real number and value of labor invested in an object, and the added or surplus jouissance value represented by an imaginary number added to the real number. The imaginary number that does not exist, in this case should be called a Real product of the imagination, rather than simply an imaginary fiction. The imaginary number (symbolic for our purposes) represents the happiness value of productive human activity. This value could be positive or negative, satisfaction or suffering. In Lacanian theory, there are different forms of surplus jouissance, and by the same token, the type of satisfaction experienced with an object may vary. In any case, loss or lack facilitates symbolic and economic exchange because no exchange can take place without it.

Conventional economic models do not address the various levels of confidence. To rebuild trust, policy makers need a credit target, aside from the conventional monetary and fiscal targets. The credit target should be the amount of credit in the economy at full employment. The amount of money as credit that is available in the system based on surplus productivity. The surplus is in the quality of the productive activity rather than the profit that comes as an added value. Credit is as good as the work of the beneficiaries of the credit, and this is what makes credit beneficent to a society. This is the speculative value that will be given to goods in the market and the stock market. This is also what Keynes referred to as animal spirits in the marketplace and Marx referred to as abstract universality (exchange value) that appears as a real substance (commodity metaphysics).

I argue that the added value of the product is its jouissance value (of which there are three). The abstract here is the singular Real value rather than the concrete exchange value for someone else. The abstract is Mind as the subjective or inward absolute value of the product for a subject. For Marx, the illusion, or metaphysics of a product, conceals the reality of a network of social relations.

This book argues that what Keynes called animal spirits in the marketplace refers not only to labor but also to the satisfaction provided by human activity and this we have said can be of various kinds. The more convenient the surplus jouissance, or the confidence generated by undivided and innovative productive activity, the stronger the credit will be circulating within the economy, and the higher stocks will rise.

I disagree with Zizek (2022) where he follows Pascal in saying that thinking can be reduced to an impersonal network of social relations in language where subjects are caught. Instead of being fascinated by a fetish, Zizek appeals to representing social relations through meaningless rituals and gestures performed in anxiety, hoping that the correct experience and belief will come by itself. The interiority of thinking and praying happens to those who already believe.

What was not considered by Zizek was Lacan's concept that thought is an unsayable form of jouissance. The thought occurs to us that the teaching may be correct because we experienced a form of jouissance in action that gave rise to a thought which confirmed the veracity of the teaching. The thought of enlightenment advances and realizes the subject.

## References

Keynes, J. M. (1935). *The General Theory of Employment, Interest, and Money.* 1488_ Keynestheroyof employment.pdf

Zizek, S. (2022). *Surplus Enjoyment: A Guide for the Non-Perplexed.* London: Bloomsbury.

# Appendix I

## An Outline of the History of the Symbolic Order or the History of Human Wisdom and Knowledge

This appendix reviews the history of the symbolic order in the West and the East and proposes four original historical hypothesis.

1   First that biblical and cultural history is the history of thought and the symbolic order, not of the material universe, and that the symbolic order evolved from the material universe in the form of an orbital leap from the semiotic to the symbolic. The semiotic regulates the exchange of signs (electrical, chemical, etc.) within the body, while the symbolic refers to thoughts and signifiers in language. Science is a symbolic form of thought about the semiotics at work in matter before symbolic thought existed. The null hypothesis is that the universe was created symbolically first or in G-d's thought as a map and the material universe was created only 6,000 years ago with a built-in history that functions retroactively. The tree, for example, was created full grown with a history in its rings. This thesis seems both ridiculous and fantastic, thus the opposite thesis must be true as determined by the Jewish Talmud mentioned below.

2   Second that the Chinese invented monotheism 2000 BCE.

3   Third that Jasper's Axial lasted longer than he thought, up to even 600 CE.

4   Fourth that Dogen (Dogen, 1200) represents the peak of the Axial age in the East in Japan in the year 1200 CE. The proposition is that true Buddha-nature is no-Buddha nature as formulated by Buddha in India, migrated to Chan in China and finally to Dogen in Japan; represents the crown jewel of Buddha's wisdom and of the *Caodong zong* school of Chan in China and Japan that survives to this day and now been transmitted to the West (*Deshimaru Roshi* in Paris and *Suzuki Roshi* in San Francisco).

The question of the age of the symbolic order is not the same as the age of rudimentary culture or religion, for example. The *Ishango* bones with natural numbers, or the know-how of hunter gatherers phase of human culture, is not the same as the question of the age of the solar system and the universe. The former is the history of human thought, the latter the history and evolution of matter. The symbolic order contains a mythical phase, a religious phase, a philosophical spiritual political phase, and a scientific phase. In contrast to Comte's (a French philosopher of the enlightenment) subdivision of Culture into primitive, religious (intermediate), and scientific (advanced), these three phases co-exist in contemporary culture as the different faces of contemporary Culture.

Are there cycles in history and evolution, and are history and evolution the same thing? Jaspers (1953) distinguishes between pre-history, ancient or traditional culture, and the Axial period. Although I agree in principle to there being three categories or periods to the history of the symbolic order, I do not necessarily divide them or conceive of them in the same way. At some point, the multiplicity of factors renders their analysis unintelligible. Is it possible to still find a pattern that can be counted with the hand? What about the multiplicity of factors, don't they prevent the possibility of finding a less complex pattern?

"Temporal limitations—such, for example, as the biblical belief in a world 6,000 years old—have been broken through. Something endless opens into the past and into the future" (Kaplan, 1981, p.xiii).

The history of symbols and the symbolic order begun 6,000 years ago, which coincides with what the Bible says about the age of the created universe. My thesis is that this is not the age of the material universe but of the symbolic order. At 6000 BC culture became an organized system and not simply isolated symbols. The second thesis is that the beginning of monotheism in China marks the birth of the symbolic order. Be that as it may, although many claim that empirically or phenomenologically, there are as many symbolic orders as there are cultures, my thesis is that the symbolic function has a common origin for all cultures.

> An organizing concept of the Axial age is the concept of a single meaningful pattern, in which all diverse cities have their appointed place. This according to Hegel is the place that history assigned to Christ. All history goes toward and comes from Christ. The appearance of the son of God is the axis of world history. But the Christian faith is only one faith, not the faith of mankind. This view of universal history therefore suffers from the defect that can only be valid for believing Christians.
>
> (Jaspers, 2012)

Hegel (1904) recapitulates the argument that he made by sketching once more the ascent of the human spirit in terms of the development of the self from sense-certainty to religion, even self-certainty about religion versus the certainty of other religions. Hegel argues that spirit must progress beyond religion, which is the making of picture-thoughts of the absolute. He argues that in the new stage of development, the contents of religion must become the contents and guide of people's actions. Hegel claims that the stage that is now being achieved is what he calls systematic science, which is a pure knowledge of the self. This systematic science has been achieved through the long and tortuous processes he has described. There can be no other way because, for Hegel, knowledge is formed through struggle and development. Hegel restates his principle as a conclusion. Systematic science has to observe the development of spirit in specific times, places, and environments. It cannot be purely theoretical or speculative. As a result, the science of spirit is in a sense the work of history and this work confirms the thesis that G-d is the ruler of history through repetition and punishment, and forgiveness and surprise. The work of the Law *(regula)* is the field of the secular world *(secula)*.

Rather I would claim that the axis of history is to be found in the period around 500 BC, in the spiritual process that occurred between 800 and 200 BCE. It is there that we meet with the deepest cut in the line of history. Humans as we know them today came into being at this time.

Instead of keeping the rules of a dead tradition by rote, the tradition must be validated in genuine lucid experience. This is not the beginning of world religions as Jaspers believed but the ongoing evolution of the tradition while simultaneously staying the same. The claim to universality appears in the particular manner of claiming universality. At this point, experience can also be distorted since experience and revelation have been used to validate the universality not of the experience but of a particular major religion as the only true religion.

Another aspect of Jasper's analysis of tradition with which this text departs from is that tradition is purely mythical in the bad sense of myth as false knowledge. This certainly would not be true of Judaism since it is highly rational and codified, and the same could be said of the Vedas.

Communion with a group and clarified experience consistent with reason launched a campaign of logos against myth and of practical or ethical reason against the unreal figures of the gods. Religion was rendered ethical, and it had to make you a better person rather than worse. The criterion was humanistic. Rational and spiritual humans found a way to raise themselves above their egos and above the Renaissance world of individualism rising at that time: "What was later called reason and personality was revealed for the first time during the axial period" (idem, p. 3).

The absolute or G-d lies in the interior without a relationship to the neighbor: the emptiness of interdependence. There is a pure interiority of the self as substance or non-substance. From Hegel's point of view the Buddhist nothingness lacks an understanding of subjectivity or personality/ego. Then according to Heidegger's terminology, needs can be formulated as either one eats or one is eaten, either one uses the 24 hours or the 24 hours use you.

The word *satori* (bodhi or enlightened body-mind) designates the state of the spirit in which the spirit flowers or blooms beyond itself and passes through a spectrum of light. For Jaspers the Axial age "melts down, assimilates or causes the old traditions to sink from view, irrespective of whether it was the same people or others that became the bearers of the new cultural forms" (idem). If you chose the old traditions instead, then you chose to stay primitive, and you either evolve with or die out the Axial. The term Axial is used because it represents a cut into the line of history indicating a change in the structure over a long period of time, not unlike evolution. A parallel is observed between human cultural history and biological human evolution.

With the advent of science out of the Axial, three currents develop over time, in my opinion. The development of science, and a "scientism" compatible with an orthodox religious tradition, but not with spirituality, and a spirituality compatible with science. Tradition continues rejecting science, including aspects of the Axial, and the Axial also critiques instrumental or unethical uses of science. Although science and technology come out of the Axial period, military weapons can render humans barbaric once again, cancelling thereby the alleged evolution from a past that did not become extinct, only hidden, perhaps like (not the same, different orbits, steps, or levels) the letters of DNA.

Before moving forward let's recapitulate the three ages discussed so far. To the three ages, I will add a fourth:

1   Tradition. Ancestors. 5000 BCE creation of a symbolic order or a human symbolic order.
2   Jaspers' Axial age from 500 BCE not to 200 CE like he claims, but to 300 or even 600 CE.
3   The Western enlightenment and its conflict with tradition and spirituality.
4   To number 3, I add the postmodern as the current time wherein all the ages are found co-existing in union and in conflict.

# 1     Tradition

Evidence of the appearance of human culture begins with the *Gobekli Tepi* 12000 BCE in Turkey. They worshipped a headless person, a phallus, and a bull. The Sumerians invented the cuneiform writing and had knowledge of geometry. Archeological evidence was found at the Sumerian *Urta* temple in the Mesopotamia (5,000 BCE). They worshipped *Ninurta* who was a God of war and fertility. All the figures of worship symbolize the primal father, the totem cylinders, and the totem animal, all consistent with Freud's view of the origin of the human horde, language, culture, and religion. The English word "fascinate", derived from the Latin *fascinum,* and the related verb *fascinare,* means to use the power of the *fascinus* or the erect phallus.

A symbolic order properly begins around 5000 BCE with the appearance of Sumerian civilization. Sumerian cuneiform script appeared 2000 years before Egyptian hieroglyphics (3000 BCE). Babylonian culture appeared 500 years after Egyptian civilization (2500 BCE) and at the same time as Ancient Indian civilization. 2000 BCE marks the appearance of Chinese civilization and of Sumerian, Egyptian, Babylonian, Aramaic, Sanskrit, and Chinese languages. None of these protolanguages survive in their original form. Aramaic evolved into Hebrew and Arabic. Egyptian hieroglyphics evolved into Hebrew letters, and Sanskrit evolved into Hindi. Hebrew, Arabic and Hindi are living languages spoken in Israel, Arab countries, and India.

According to Cassirer (Cassirer, 1946, p.20), philological research can trace the process leading to the development of a symbolic mind representative of a human symbolic order. Animals already had senses and reflexes, but in humans they are employed through a symbolic function. But the meaning conferred unto sense experience includes aspects of experience that cannot be attributed to either intellect or sense experience. Monkeys have intellect and signs but no symbolic function. Lemurs can use symbols to perform complicated computations, and yet they don't have predicate language. Sense, or meaning, is more than the senses and includes bodily experience as well. The symbolic determines experience, and at the same time, Real experience includes something undetermined outside symbolization. Exploring the traces of vanished times, we can experience our ancestors and find in ourselves the strings that link us to ancient times. Names and language had to appear before any principle or deity could be named.

It is interesting that Cassirer (1964) book documents the history of religious thought, if religion is the correct word since at the time it represents all there was. According to Cassirer, the earliest form of religion is the mana concept as a One power present in things or a force field that permeates everything. Such power is considered sacred, while its negative aspect remains taboo.

The taboo mana formula has been regarded as the minimum definition of religion, i.e., as the expression of a distinction which constitutes one of the essential, indispensable conditions of religious life as such, and represents the lowest level of it that we know.

(p.64)

Cassirer believes that the concept of one "G-dhead" receives its first development through language. However, there's no reason that any unity should prevail in language except in the form of how it requires a battery of discreet and diacritical signifiers and terms functioning in unison as a structure. This principle must be accepted as a minimum definition of language. Otherwise, language tends towards division, displacement, discrimination, and metonymy. A symbolic order is not the same as Imaginary ideology. It has laws, stories, Names, and ancestral history.

According to Lacan, metaphor is the form of language that holds language together. Within metaphor it's the paternal metaphor otherwise known as the Name of the Father that has a libidinal component represented by the desire of the mother (*mana-mama-mammal*).

In a Freudian formulation, a totem contains both a positive power and a negative power. The negative fear inducing power is linked to a taboo against the killing of the father or other siblings, but it also represents the emotional power of love that unifies them and allows them to project their own aggression towards the totem and fear the totem instead of each other. They can now love each other as once they loved the father. Thus, I argue that the unity of language is predicated on bonds of love. The love of the mother towards the child and the father or towards the name of the father in language is guided by the force of love in language,

> The mythic mind finally reaches a point where it is no longer contented with the variety, abundance and concrete fullness of divine attributes and names, but where it seeks to attain, through the unity of the word, the unity of the G-d idea. But even here man's mind does not rest content. Beyond this unity, it strives for a concept of Being that is unlimited by any manifestation, and therefore not expressible in any word, not called by any name.
>
> (Cassirer, p.73)

This paragraph of Cassirer, except for the totemic phase and science, cuts across the entire history of religious thought up to the present time. While animal species existed before language, in contrast to us, they move through their world without predicate language as through a dark sea, or as if we moved through a sea of brightness without being able to discern forms with the help of language. And as we discern, recognize, and invent our object world, with the help of language, the background of light and darkness is transformed into an alternating contrast between chaos and creation. Chaos like the Real can both disrupt and facilitate the emergence of structure. For the Babylonians it was language that transformed Chaos into an organized matrix of being.

It is interesting that early Egyptian texts, before Judaism (perhaps two knowledge trends co-joined in Moses, the Hebrew Egyptian), had the concept of a hidden G-d that functions as the dark matrix of creation. This hidden G-d had no form, image, or name (not even the name of the nameless) that we know of, until the Chinese and the Hebrews gave it a name. For the Egyptians it was a pure form of Being without representation. For the Chinese and the Hebrews, the hidden G-d is revealed in language and beyond language. The hidden unknown G-d survives in the Romans as one of their deities. Paul appealed to the Romans in the Name of this G-d and agreed with the Epicureans and Stoics of that time who taught that G-d is spirit and self-sufficiency. However, the Romans would not accept the resurrection as evidence of the godliness of Jesus. The evidence of G-dliness was in his enlightened heart that bore the crucifixion and was resurrected. The resurrection requires faith not evidence or logos.

We find a similar case in the Bible. In the psalms (18:12) we read: "He made darkness his Hiding place. Then in another psalm (139:12) it is written: "Even darkness is not dark to you. Night shines like day – light and darkness are the same".

This is not that different from the late phases of religious thought up to this day. The only name or denotation that remains for the real One is the expression of negation: its own non-Being. Being in emptiness is revealed in the One saying, "No, no; above 'This' there is nothing else". This shows a kind of circularity or eternal return from the early to the late forms of symbolic thought (consistent with Eliade's and Nietzsche's view of the eternal return). Deleuze underscores that a principle of the will here eliminates anything reactive as far as the eternal recurrence and becoming of being is concerned. Here Deleuze accepts an absolute spirit of negation to negate the compulsive repetition of the same (Parr, 2005, p.87). Deleuze is not that far from the Buddhist distinction between the wheel of Karma and Samsara and the wheel of the Dharma. Only the latter repeats with a constructive difference.

After Egyptian hieroglyphics, Phoenician, Sumerian, Aramaic, and Sanskrit, Chinese language appears under the legendary yellow emperor (2700 BCE). Chinese is historically documented with the Shia dynasty around 2100 BCE (300 years before Abraham). Simplified Chinese of course is spoken to this day and uses traditional Chinese for its background. Sanskrit appears much earlier than Hinduism and the Vedas. Only later does it become linked the Vedas and Hinduism (1500 BCE).

Abraham appears around 1800 BCE most likely speaking Aramaic. The traditional Jewish understanding was that Chinese monotheism comes after Abraham. In the biblical text, it says that G-d gave other people gifts equivalent to Abrahamic monotheism. The temporal sequence here is probably incorrect. It is shocking to discover that the Chinese invented monotheism not Abraham.

The earliest references to *Shang Di* are found in oracle bone inscriptions of the Shang Dynasty in the third millennium BC, although the later work Classic of History claims yearly sacrifices were made to Shang Di by Emperor Shun (2700 BCE), even before the Xia Dynasty. Of course, that the *Ishango* bones are older and have been dated to be 20,000 years ago. The bones have notches carved in groups. Some groups are prime numbers

In fact, the evidence seems to indicate that Chinese monotheism was prior to Abraham and that Abraham in fact may have been influenced by Chinese monotheism. The original Chinese One (*Shang D*i) was monotheistic although Taoism is both monotheistic and polytheistic, and Confucianism and Buddhism are nontheistic. At least when G-d spoke to Abraham, the Infinite light unknowingly knew that it had already revealed itself as *Shang Di* for the Chinese people, and now YHVH was creating a new tradition, people, and lineage with Abraham and then again with Ishmael. In this sense the Axial age did not invent a new tradition, but simply the Axial age represents a refraction of the same Light unto a different tradition or lineage.

However, to make matters worse and to throw a monkey wrench on a theory of a neat separation between periods and modes of understanding, China's *Shang Di 's* Temple of Heaven was only built 1406 CE at the same time as the forbidden city in Beijing. It would be worthwhile for world peace that religious leaders of the five major religions meet at the Temple of Heaven in Beijing (by permission of the Chinese government) for a ceremony of world peace. The Temple Mount and the Al Aqsa Mosque are very similar in design and color to the Temple of Heaven. Once an agreement is reached, a temple rock from the Temple of Heaven could be used ceremoniously as a Torah, Chan, and Gospel representatives to lay the foundation for the Third Jewish Temple as a house of prayer and meditation for all people. The courtyard would feature a statue of a bull, of Moses, Jesus, and Buddha where all people could congregate before the holy of holies.

The appearance of written Hebrew coincides with Moses and the receiving of the Torah at Mount Sinai (1313 BCE). The first temple in Jerusalem was built 1000 BCE or 200 years after Moses or 800 years after Abraham. It was destroyed in 827 BCE. The second temple was built in 349 BCE and destroyed 69 CE after Christ.

## 2    The Axial Age

As we see, tradition has brought us from 5000 BCE to the common era. In this sense, tradition lasted longer than the Jaspers Axial age seemed to indicate or in other words, the Axial age began in 500 BCE and took 500 years to be established and cemented itself before it began to interact and make profound changes in the tradition.

The concept of Law is another vantage point from which to consider the history of the symbolic order. Tradition in this sense would go back further into the second millennium after the birth of the symbolic order. The laws and covenant of Noah (that the bible sets at 5000 BC) prescribe a legal system to handle ordinary human problems. Here the Law is associated with the establishment of spiritual and social peace. Although the concept of a legal system originates in resolving practical conflicts among individuals, the concept of law had a spiritual perspective and played an important part in cosmology, religion, politics, personal conduct, and philosophy and has an infinite range of meanings all the way to the no-meaning of emptiness or the Law of emptiness.

Currently in the legal system, the spiritual concept of law has vanished from the courts, except by the presence of G-d in the holy writ as the guarantor of truth. A subject must swear upon the bible to say the truth and nothing but the truth ("so help me G-d"). Many consider this as an archaism that has no place in the legal system and should be relegated to the realm of poetry and philosophy. The purpose of the reference is purely historical and merely represents a binding of obligation for the members of society. The law signifies an order that is valid and binding to the members of society. Roman Law, for example, as a form of civilization, respecting the idea of a fair trial and the rights of the individual, was rejected by Hitler and the Nazi's as Semitic and therefore could not stop them from crafting and executing their final solution upon the Jews.

During the Axial age, we find *Lao Tzi* and *Kong Tzi* in China, the Buddha in India, the Greek philosophers in Greece, and the prophets in Israel. These teachers will have a profound influence in history that would last according to some two hundred to three hundred years into the common area and according to others to the year 600 of the common era.

The Axial age seems to last longer than previously observed (500–200 BCE) because it goes from 500 BCE to at least 300 CE with the appearance of Nagarjuna the same year as Christ, and *Vasubandhu* and Yogacara Buddhism supplementing the Mahayana's second turning of the Dharma wheel, in the year 300 CE. In the next 300 years, Chan will be established in China and Mohammed appears in the Middle East.

While Chan in China develops the Axial age in the Tang dynasty and Christianity in the West, Mohammed attempts to re-write tradition by force if necessary. Both Christianity and Islam share a defiance of Jewish Law based on the non-acceptance by the Jews of either Jesus or Mohammed as the Messiah. Christianity replaces the Torah with a new Gospel, while the Koran replaces the Torah not with something new, or different content, but with new timelines, ethnicities, language, and characters for the same thing.

In Pauline Christianity, the chosenness of Christ is proven by the resurrection, while for the Jews the evidence of their chosenness is proven by the collective receiving of the Torah at Mount Sinai. For Christ's resurrection we have a witness in Mary Magdalene. There are also visions of Jesus, but these do not prove the resurrection and/or that there is life after death. For the Torah we have the evidence of Torah itself whether it was received by inspiration of the Holy Spirit, whether in thought or word. The Gospels are the recordings of the sayings of Jesus as a personification not of G-d, as believed by Christians, but of the Holy Spirit (*Ruach Hakodesh*). Jesus did not say that the Torah was for a future era, but that it was being misunderstood, and he presents an actualized version for the same teachings and principles.

Shortly after the death of Mohammed, Sufism appears as a spiritual lineage of Islam which then may be seen as compatible with the Axial age. Otherwise, Muhammad represents the one exception to the Axial age in the attempt to return to some form of ancestral culture while simultaneously entering into conflict and war with the textual source of the Koran in Judaism. Muhammed wrote a Torah for the sons of Ishmael. "Jewish religious law places Islam within the realm of the adulteration of the Torah with non-Jewish elements" (Schoeps, 1963, p.16). Traditional culture, which existed for 5,000 years, now co-exists with symbols of the Axial age and the scientific age of rational enlightenment. In another similar contemporary example, now Hinduism claims Buddhism as part of Hinduism in the form of the non-dual Vedanta teaching that emerged much later and under the influence of Buddhism.

The Axial age also seems to have a pivot right in the middle with the beginning of the common era with Christ and Nagarjuna who ushered new developments with the Gospel and the non-dual Dharma as a new teaching rather than a presentation of the same older tradition. The Koran is a Torah for the lineage of Ishmael as was promised in the Bible (the Koran is a different cultural form of the Torah but does not represent a new teaching).

In addition, the Axial age did not stop traditions from continued development. In fact, the opposition between Judaism and Christianity, between law and love, between observance of the Sabbath by rote and the spiritual experience of the Sabbath is not so. The Rabbis taught that the Sabbath is delivered into the hand of the person and not the person into an oppressive law of the Sabbath. The same is the case with the observance of the Law (works). Although there are 613 commandments, a whole-hearted observance of a single commandment not only fulfills the entire Torah but also causes the Holy Spirit to rest upon the person. Thus, while the Lubavitcher Rebbe claimed that outreach to the larger community would hasten the coming of Mashiach, this was already stated in the Talmud. Traditional Jewish books such as the Mishna and the Talmud appeared during this time, although they are attributed to ancient biblical sources.

Arabs conquer Jerusalem and 600 years later they conquered India and arrogantly and violently help destroy Buddhism in India. During those 600 years Buddhism was transmitted to China and Tibet, and then the destruction of Buddhism in India by the Muslims coincided with the temporary decline of Buddhism in China and the revival of Taoism and Confucianism. Another way of seeing it is that Chan preserved Buddhism through the amalgamation of Taoism, Confucianism, and Buddhism in China. At the same time, Crusaders conquered Jerusalem.

Mohammed made some errors in relating certain events of the Torah in the Koran. He placed Pharaoh, Haman, and the creation of the Tower of Babel all in one period (*Sura* 28:38) when the periods in which these people lived were thousands of years apart. He also writes that Mary, the supposed mother of Jesus (*Sura* 19:28), was the sister of Aaron (and Moses) and that *Imram* (Amram) was their father (*Sura* 66:12). The prophetess Miriam lived thousands of years before Mary. Mohammed exposed himself as the creator of a man-made book of laws that in essence copied the Torah.

His religion spread mostly by force, and that's how he got the masses to "believe in him". However, the actual ideas and the general practices were all quite easy to implement because of the Arabs' tremendous exposure to the surrounding Jewish communities.

Chan and Mahayana Buddhism survived by amalgamation in Japan and Korea, while Theravada Buddhism, also of the Axial age, and the *Nikaya* sutras continue unabated. So, we see that the Axial age itself is also comprised of traditionalists and innovators. My third thesis is that the peak of the Axial age in the East is Dogen in Japan in the year 1200 CE.

The period of the Tang dynasty as a golden age of Chinese Culture in the East coincided with the dark middle ages in Europe from 400 CE to 1200. It is noteworthy that no mathematical knowledge (the Queen of the sciences) was produced in Europe during this time. It was the Muslims who introduced advanced Greek and Indian mathematical knowledge during the dark ages in Europe.

Then around the same time in Spain we also have representatives of tradition (Maimonides) as well as the new spirituality of the Kabbalah (mystical Jewish tradition) and the Aristotelean formalization of Christianity by Aquinas in Italy. Jewish Law is codified in Spain by Joseph Karo from Toledo and who later dies in Tzefat, the home of the Kabbalah in Israel. As the mystical Kabbalah ushers forth, the tradition of the Law or Halacha also grows.

## 3

The next marker for my analysis is the Western enlightenment, the publication of the *Shobogenzo* (the Eye and Treasury of the True Law) for the first time in Japan (400 years later after Dogen's death), the appearance of the *Baal Shem Tov* (master of the good name), wholehearted Hassidism in Judaism, the American and French revolutions of the 1700s, and the publication of Smith's *The Wealth of Nations*. All these developments in the areas of religion, science, and government are representative of the Axial age, and Hassidism represents a renewal of the Jewish tradition with an emphasis on the spiritual and Kaballah that balanced the rationalism of Reform Judaism. Hassidism represents a spiritual approach to traditional Judaism, while Haskalah (enlightenment Judaism) is the new rationalistic perspective.

The eighteenth century ushers into the rational enlightenment and the development of government and society. Science and modernity conflict with tradition although they virtually adopt the values of the Axial age for its modern spirituality. The periods of the symbolic order, including prehistory, nowadays are found intermixed and nervously co-existing in postmodernity.

If I were to place what I have said thus far in a Borromean knot of four, the symbolic would be Judaism and Hinduism, the Real would be Buddhism and Christianity, the Imaginary would be Islam, and the Sinthome or second Real organizing the knot would be the Chinese monotheism of *Shang Di.*

Given that I have claimed that the Biblical age of the Universe is the age of the symbolic order, including the Axial and scientific ages, and not the age of the material universe that was created first. The symbolic order evolved from the created material universe as Darwin predicted.

Rabbi Aryeh Kaplan wrote an essay on Kabbalah and the age of the Universe. He was a rabbi with an MA in Physics. In it, he wrote:

> Whoever or whatever created the carbon atom specifically designed it so that it would, under certain conditions, be able to build amino acids and proteins. From the animate to the inanimate. From solid crystals and minerals to the creation of biological life.

(p.16)

In very primitive life, magnified fatty amino acids that aren't alive, but critical for life, are like soap bubbles adding water to fatty acids, and this causes them to self-assemble into round vesicles or containers, perfect for holding and protecting cell functions and DNA information. A container or membrane, or what Lacan called a Real sack is the first step for creating life.

> According to Kaplan there are several viewpoints on how to reconcile science with the Torah or traditional Jewish wisdom. "For example, when God created a tree, he created it with rings – i. e. with its history; so, to with all of creation. Since G-d is different, he can create a world which has its history inherent in it from the moment of creation".

(Idem, p. 21)

According to science, the modern human form came into existence about 100,000 years ago. From subhuman primates to the first humans, this change happened 100,000 years ago. Then 12,000 years ago *Gobekli Tepi* in Turkey reflects the results and evidence of this evolution. *Tepi* has the oldest temple, and they worshiped a headless person, the bull, and an erect phallus, consistent with Freud's scientific myth that demonstrates the transition from the subhuman primate to the human.

Following the Jewish tradition, Kaplan assumes that there were 974 generations that lived before Adam who lived for the full 1,000 years that Adam was intended to live. The Bible says that Adam and Eve had a child when they were 130 years old. This would mean that if we accept the Jewish proposition of there being 974 generations before Adam that lived for 1,000 years, the first human forms came into existence 100,000 years ago in line with current scientific thought. The Talmud asserts the existence of 974 generations that existed before Adam derived from a biblical verse where G-d commanded something for 1000 generations.

Both the Midrash and the Talmud teach that one of the days of G-d is equal to 1,000 of our years. Of course, this is a mythical assumption rather than a logical one. A year in the earth is equivalent to a day in the life of the Universe. Thus, one of the years of G-d is 1,000 x 365 days or 365,000 years.

At the time of creation, the world was already 42,000 years old. Before his creation we use divine years not human ones. Therefore, the age of the universe is 42,000 divine years. As we have explained one divine year is equal to 365,000 human years. Therefore, the age of the universe in human years is 42,000 x 365,000 – i.e., close to 15 billion years old which is what science best estimate is of how old the universe is.

(p. 35)

Is it possible that the creation of the universe took place over 13 billion years ago as science says, and that very much later, less than 5,000 years ago, the symbolic order evolved from matter in between the time of the creation of the solar system and the time of the creation of the earth 4.6 billion years ago.

Was the first creation created in thought, or in material extension, to use Descartes' categories? In the Talmud, there are two accounts: that the world was created in September or *Tishri* for Rosh Hashana and that the world was created in the lunar month of *Nissan* (Tohu and Bohu). Reconciling these two perspectives, as the Talmud often does, we get the result that the world was created in *Nissan*, while in *Tishri* the world was created in thought. The creation of the world in Nissan coincides with the creation of the Universe first in *Tishri* and then followed much later by the creation of the symbolic order in *Nissan*.

I argue that the creation of the world in thought represents the creation of the symbolic order. The 5,000 years of the Bible represent the period of the creation of a symbolic order. But the world was first created in matter, and then at some point out of matter evolved the world of thought and the symbolic order.

Or is it the other way around? Is it that the creation in thought took place 13 billion years ago and 6,000 years later G-d created it in actuality? This is the naïve view that the age of the symbolic order is the same as the age of the Universe. First came the thought of the symbolic order or the map and then came the creation of the territory. I believe in reality, it's the other way around.

In the end, Jewish thought concurs with science's dating of the age of the universe (i.e., scientific evidence in fact, as opposed to scientific philosophy). The conflicts posed by science have been discussed by Jewish sages centuries ago, and by maintaining a firm grounding in these holy texts, we can see that all these conflicts have been resolved.

The atom becomes visible when there is a release of energy when the electron jumps from one orbit to another. When electrons leap, the loss of energy has a fixed definite value. A leap between primates and humans may be akin to a leap between material and symbolic universes, between matter and thought, in the same way that the electron leaps in space-time from one order to another. The energy is kept constant at a fixed value, rather than eventually dissipating into a cold material ocean of tranquility.

Another ancient Sumerian myth is that hiding behind the planets Uranus and Neptune (which they already had discovered 9,000 years before us) there is a tenth planet in the solar system from where an advanced civilization sent spaceships to earth. To facilitate agriculture, they decided to build a new species to help them cultivate the earth. Advanced genetic techniques were used to combine the genes of apes and humans. This is something that science 9,000 years had learned to do but could not execute for ethical reasons. Apes who did not have kings were considered red barbarians. Those who had kings were the ancestors of black-faced humans.

Just as it is helpful to think of a leap in time between primates and humans with the discovery of language and the symbolic order, we find an analogical leap between the orbits of the electrons that prevents them from falling into the entropy that affects the planets in orbit around the sun. Unlike matter, the thought of enlightenment, like the particles that emerge from the void, and the void or universe itself, cannot be destroyed.

## Appendix to the Appendix

Table of the history of the symbolic order

| | |
|---|---|
| Egyptian Hieroglyphics | 3100 |
| Aramaic | 3000 |
| Phoenician, Sumerian | 3000 |
| Sanskrit | 3000–1700 |
| Yellow Emperor | 2700 BC |
| Earliest **Chinese** | 2000 |
| Xia Dynasty | 2100 documented |
| Abraham | 2000 |
| Shang Dynasty | 1600 |
| Rig Vedas | 1500 |
| *Tutenkamon* | 1336 BC |
| Hebrew | 1300 |
| Ramses II | 1304 |
| Moses | 1200 |
| Buddha/Kong *Lao Tzi* | 500 BC |
| Kong Tzi | |
| Prophets | |
| Jesus/Nagarjuna | 0 CE |
| Vasubhandu | 300 CE |
| Bodhidharma | 400 CE |
| Kumarajiva | 400 |
| Nagarjuna | |
| Muhamed | 620 |
| Tang Dynasty | 618–907 |
| Huayen Chinese Buddhism | 620 |
| Xuanzang | 630 |
| Yogachara | |
| Heart Sutra | |
| *Hui Neng* Chinese Buddhism | 676 |
| Dongshan | 807–869 |
| *T'ien-t'ai* Chinese Buddhism | 794–1185 |
| *Hung Chi* | 1091–1157 |
| Last *Caodong* | |
| Master in China that survived great persecution | |

| | |
|---|---|
| Chan survived the chaos of five dynasties and was used by Song dynasty and the entire population. Five houses and Tang teachers officially recognized. Lin chi school dominates | |
| Muslims invade India and help destroy Nalanda University and Buddhism in India | 1200 |
| Dogen in Japan | 1223 |

# References

Cassirer, E. (1946). *Language and Myth*. New York: Dover Publications.

*Dogen* (1200). *Shobogenzo*. Tokyo: Weatherhill.

Friedan, B. (1974). The Feminine Mystique, New York: Dell Publishers.

Hegel, G.H.F. (1904). *The Phenomenology of the Spirit*. London: Cambridge University Press, 2003.

Jaspers, K. (1953). *The Origin and Goal of History*. New York: Routledge, 2021.

Jaspers, K. (2012). *The Axial Age and its Consequences*. Cambridge: The Belknap Press of Harvard University Press.

Kaplan, A. (1981). *The Infinite Light*. New York: The National Conference of Synagogue Youth.

Kaplan, A. (2007). *Kabbalah and the Age of the Universe*. New York: The National Conference of Synagogue Youth.

Schoeps, H. (1963). *The Jewish-Christian Argument*. New York: Hold, Rinehart, and Winston.

# Appendix II

## Theory of the Libido and Lacan's Three Jouissances: Freud, Jung, Bion, and Lacan

Freud's metapsychology has a metaphor of the Psyche/drive and the Mind/ defenses in Freud. The mind is divided and unified at the same time. Jung does not distinguish between a psychical instinct and a sublime drive. In addition, he does not understand the difference between instinct and drive, compulsion and Tyche, or repetition with a difference. Division and unity can be pathological or unified. Unity can be healthy or pathological: Bion's 'O' is more or less Lacan's second Real. The Mind and the Psyche are fundamentally divided among animal instinct, human law, empty spirit, and reason.

The Psyche and Mind are both One and Other. Energy or libido was sexual for Freud and *a*sexual for Jung. Jung's approach seems more scientific since scientists don't ordinarily get sexually aroused by particles. For Lacan, the libido is a form of Eros and death drive. For Jung the libido was *a*sexual, a form of Platonic Agape, and the One of the occult, while for Lacan the One was based on the history of philosophy. For Jung the libido is generally *a*sexual and specifically sexual in eroticism. For Freud the libido is particularly sexual while generally non-sexual.

Lacan incorporates Freud and Jung. The drives were monistic for Jung, while dualistic for Freud. To Freud's drive theory, Lacanian theory adds three forms of jouissance at work in the drives, but mostly on the side of the death drive that regenerates, rather than destroy the life drive. The fusion with the mother is the first jouissance of the Other. The child is an '*objet a*' for the mother, an *a*sexual object, and phallic object all at once. The phallic jouissance is the second jouissance, and the Third jouissance of the Other which itself has three forms: the feminine jouissance, the mystic jouissance, and the Third jouissance of meaning. Meaning here is Real, in the form of the enigma, and paradoxical meaning.

Jung confused the preconscious or unconscious in a descriptive sense, with the personal unrepressed unconscious which he equated with conscious repression due to social morality. Only the archetypes are inherited and collective to the species. This flies on the face of the truth that stories are presented as fiction that function as semblance for a mathematical structure. The collective are Plato's geometrical theory of five solid "archetypal" forms. Oedipus is a mathematical structure that appears in the different theories and cultural forms. The Universal within the relative, rather than the Universal being the relative.

Jung goes on to say that Freud recognizes archaic vestiges, but he objects that Freud only thinks of them in personalistic terms. The murder of the father and the totem are a universal structure that is re-experienced repeatedly in each life. It is through the totem that the aggressive drive is sublimated, but in some cases sublimation functions automatically as a direct drive without involving conscious moral repression. The drive is not a subliminal appendix to the conscious mind.

Jung accepts that the subject is bisexual or made of Yin and Yang, masculine and feminine, and he develops an androgynous ideal of sameness for males and females that persuaded the feminist movement to be androgynous and wear pants at work. Not that wearing pants is a sign of androgyny. For Freud's part, the phallus is a signifier of social difference, and without the cultural symbolic, there would be no reproduction or species. But the phallus is not a signifier of omnipotent dominion over women, and instead is the signifier of a lack. Just like black holes are organized and place planets in orbit around the sun, the psyche is not whole or All. The All always includes a hole of emptiness at its center. The symbolic phallus is both a phallus and a vagina, but this differs from androgyny. In men the symbolic phallus supports the imaginary phallus that is used sexually for sex. The imaginary phallus is the erect phallus that represents the flaccid penis. The vagina is the absence of the imaginary phallus.

In RSI, or the Borromean knot, the psyche is both divided and unified in the knot of three. In the Lacanian Borromean knot of four, the sinthome, or holy person, is what ties the knot together. In Confucian Chinese history, *Shang di* is the G-d of light and of intellectual enlightenment or insight. *Shang di* was the pure monotheistic G-d of *Lao Tzi* 1,200 years before Abraham. This teaching continues 3.600 years later with the Soto Zen teaching of *Dong-shan* of "Just This". One of the translations of YHVH is "Just This I am". This refers to "Just This". *Shang di* was 1,200 before Abraham's monotheism. "Just this" is equivalent to the Buddhist state of meditation or Chan. The Chinese invented monotheism contrary to biblical belief. This continuity is supported by anthropological and archeological record and evidence.

Jung wants to be a modern scientist studying the ancient Psyche. He thinks down the paths laid down by Ludwig Feuerbach's hypothesis of religion as "Projection". Jung recognizes that the word God has become a something devoid of a mystery, and thus, people should wash their mouths after they stated *(enunciated)* the word G-d. This god is a projection. Instead, he proposes that G-d is the mystery of mysteries and in this he agrees with Lacan and Bion. Jung was the first to use the term unconscious knowing. I have translated Lacan's *L'insu qui sait,* as unknown knowing, and in this we all agree.

In Bion's theory, Myth, Pre-conceptions, Concepts, and deductive thought are all alpha psychical elements, but he does not say they are representatives of the drive. These symbolic elements are alpha elements just like the desire of the mother is not a function, but a desire that is a signified of the Name of the Father (NoF). For Jung, archetypes are the spiritual (psychical) representatives of the drive and language for Jung only has semiotic elements or signs, just like biological signs. Jouissance with the *objet a* for Lacan is the affective representative or the drive. Jouissance is beyond signs and at the same time inscribed not within signs but signifiers.

We see how Freud, Jung, and Bion's theories are addressing the same ontological issues and realities while differing on significant points. But what about Moncayo's thought? Moncayo represents the view that Jung and Bion for the most part can be incorporated into Lacanian theory to arrive at unified psychoanalytic field theory for the twenty-first century.

We don't need yet another psychoanalytic theory, nor an integration that erases necessary differences. Although my body of work justifies a new approach, I don't present my work as such. I follow Lacan, in how he invented on the basis of Freud's work, but did not declare it a new approach, like Fromm (humanistic psychoanalysis), Klein, or Winnicott did (object relations theory). In the same way, I don't declare my reading of Lacan a new theory, but a true return to Lacan. The advantage of this approach is that it privileges psychoanalysis. When either you or I win or lose, although we lose, psychoanalysis wins.

Psychological science does psychological research on the Cartesian complex that Descartes discovered while looking at the cloth ceiling of his bed. On it, he saw a point, a line, and another line.

Instead, non-Euclidian geometry relies on the complex plane built with imaginary numbers (i). The diacritical line 0.5 is where the non-trivial zeros are found. Non-trivial zeros are equivalent to the concept of Buddhist emptiness. There we can measure an exact number for the zero that documents the level of exact quantum fluctuation around a concept of absolute zero. There we obtain a precise measurement of the alpha health elements and states of mind of a subject. We may ask what the level of absence and quantum fluctuation is in a subject at the point of entry in and exit from analysis? How can this be measured? Is this any different than measuring levels of anxiety or depression? I will return to this.

In the Cartesian plane, we measure an exact number for the negative emptiness and false zeros of pathology, for example, a depression or anxiety scale from 1 to 5. Negative emptiness of absence has an exact number of quantum fluctuations of beta elements of paranoia, anxiety, and depression. But do we interpret the quantum fluctuation as different from the symptoms? The quantum fluctuation represents the question of desire and of the desire of the Other, and its jouissance, and of a subject recognizing itself as the object cause of the other's desire.

The quantum fluctuations of the psyche are the effect of a function defined as follows:

$$f\left(x\right) = x^2$$

"f" is the name of the Function
x is the input – Argument
$x^2$ is the output – Value

Formula 1 shows the mathematical function of f(x) as well as the inputs and outputs (Graphs 1 and 2).

We may wonder why is that? In Seminar V, Lacan says (1957–1958):

> It is not just frustration as such, (...); it is the way that the subject has aimed at, has located this desire of the other which is the mother's desire, and with respect to this desire it is to make him recognize, or pass, or propose to become with respect to something which is an X of desire in the mother, to become or not the one who responds, to become or not be the desired being.

> (12.03.58, pp.3–4)

Let's compare the diagrams above based on the complex plane with the simple Cartesian plane applied to the second traditional model of both primary and secondary repression (Graph 3).

A more complex version of the same graph follows (Graph 4):

In the Cartesian plane, the positive ego ideal values are represented by the y Cartesian axis. The negative x axis is the horizon of the super-ego and the forbidden drives, and the positive ego ideal is y axis. In the complex plane, the vertical y axis is an imaginary number that represents differentiations

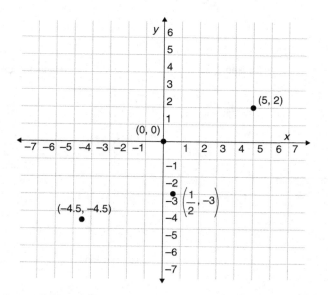

*Graph 1* Cartesian plane. Both x axis and y axis are real axis. All the numbers are real numbers. Examples of x adapted from Math World (accessed December 24, 2022).

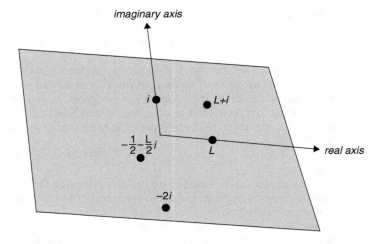

*Graph 2* Complex plane. x axis is real axis, y is Imaginary, and i is Real. All the numbers are complex numbers. Those that lie along the imaginary axis are purely imaginary, and those that lie along real axis are purely real. Adapted from Erickson C., (2005). Primary source Math World.

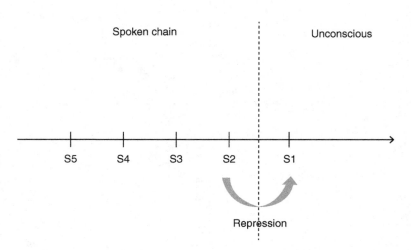

*Graph 3* Adapted from Dor 's use of the Cartesian plane (1997) to explain the theory of repression.

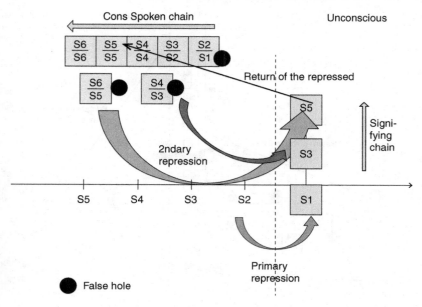

*Graph 4* Adapted from Dor, idem (1997). The Graph shows the chain or conscious suppression and the chain of unconscious repression.

within the Real unconscious and not in the symbolic Ucs. Pcs. system. But how could this be since the Real has no differentiations?

In psychosis, symbolic differentiations have not been established. In spiritual enlightenment, differentiations have been accepted and transcended. How can we get numbers from the Real? Well for mathematicians this would not be a problem since for them the Real, as distinct from reality, is mathematical. For Lacan the Real was both mystical and mathematical (mystical realism – an immaterial thought [jouissance] accurately reflects reality). If a symbolic thought or Idea in this case is an accurate concept, so the terms idealism and realism no longer apply.

How can this be so? Well, the differentiations of mathematics, more so than language, are differentiations that are not imaginary discriminations. Discriminations on the basis of the Oneness of fantasy have become the differentiations and unity of wisdom, both in science and in religion (the distinction between religion and science no longer applies here either).

Such differentiations are exactly represented by numbers. The Real has empty differentiations. This is what we mean by non-trivial zeros in the critical line. Out of these Real differentiations come the prime numbers that are

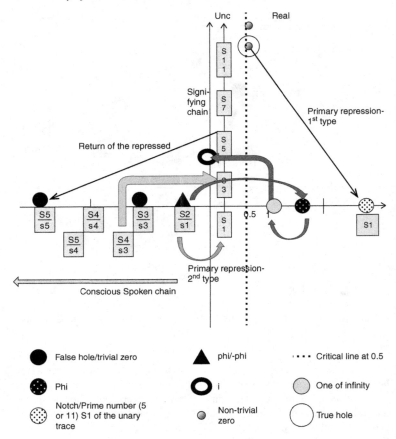

*Graph 5* The interaction of the complex and Cartesian planes applied to the theory of repression. It show the true and false holes and the trivial and not trivial zeros in which the prime numbers appear.

the basic building blocks of reality. Sublimation is measured in the complex plane by imaginary numbers in the i axis. The first symbolic element was a set. The elements of the set are constituted as a unit that contains zero. That macro set constructed a human symbolic and represented a bridge among bodily signs and linguistic and auditive signifiers (Graph 5).

The analytical task is how to transform the false hole of the repressive and repressed, for the true hole of form. Signifiers acquire a different jouissance available on the i axis, and the subject's life becomes re-organized.

Lacan draws the same circle that we draw on the complex plane. In the Seminar on the Sinthome, session of the 11th of May of 1976, Lacan says that the infinite straight line is the best illustration of the hole within the circle. He draws a circle around what for us would be $1/-1$ and i $/-i$. This circle unites the values of the repressed unconscious with the values of the Real unconscious resulting in a therapeutic effect that can be measured (Graph 6).

Later in the same seminar Lacan links the infinite line with the concept of the Unconscious.

"One knows things that that have to do with the signifier; the old notion of the Unconscious, of the *Unbekannte*, was precisely something based on our ignorance of what is happening in our bodies. But Freud's Unconscious, is something that is worthwhile stating on this occasion, it is precisely what I said. Namely, the relationship, the relationship between a body which is foreign to us which is a circle, indeed an infinite straight line, which in any case are one and the other equivalent, and something which is the Unconscious." Lacan, Seminar XXIII. The Sinthome.

(Session of May 11, 1976, pp.1–10)

We ignore the microprocesses taking place in the unconscious body. Lacan (1958a) says that

the presence of the signifier in the Other is, in effect, a presence usually closed to the subject, because it usually persists in a state of repression, and because from there it insists on representing itself in the signified by means of its repetition compulsion.

(p.200)

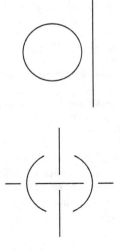

*Graph 6* The Circle and the Infinite Line are parallel and then inside each other.

It is well represented in Graph 6 above by the red arrow that goes underneath the x axis and that shows primary repression (2nd type). The $S_1$ there is the imaginary phallus, which is the signified of the NoF (Name of the Father) and is repressed under primary repression in the Freudian unconscious (Ucs). In the complex plane, the $S_1$ of the repressed Freudian unconscious is found between 0 and 0.5. So the arrow goes from –phi (–0.618...) to somewhere between 0 and 0.5. But this is no longer the Freudian, but the Lacanian unconscious. In the complex plane we have said that the Freudian unconscious appears in the real axis. As the formula reminds us in the process of repression, there is the unknown and immeasurable remainder left that Lacan marks as U. For us, U, rather than O in Bion, signifies the Real unconscious. The Real unconscious shows the mind as matter and emptiness as form. The Unconscious is not only the unknown O but also unknown in the form of an equation (U).

$$\frac{S2}{S1} \cdot \frac{S1}{s1} \to S2\left(\frac{U}{s1}\right)$$

$$-1 \times (-0,618...) = 0,5 \times U$$

Formula 2 is explained in the paragraph below.

$-1 \times (-0,618...) = 0,5 \times U$ means that in speech there is always something missing, an emptiness or the formal parrot speech that says nothing yet and is a form of auditive and enigmatic jouissance. U for universe is like the swastika at the center of mind and at the center of the Cartesian and complex planes. Swastika is not the same as the Nazi symbol, as it is an ancient Buddhist symbol. The swastika has an additional two hands that turn inward and outward. In the Nazi symbol, the hands are inverted and are turning outward first instead of inward.

If we turn $\frac{U}{S1}$ into a binary matrix, where we have two universes and two master signifiers, the true master is represented as $-S_1$ as an imaginary number.

Graphs 5 and 7 are very dense and we would like to explain especially the graph 5 step by step. Please look at the simplified version below (Graph 7):

Colette Soler says (2006),

> At the end of analysis when the subject has zeroed in on her symptom's absolute difference, there can arise not a limitless love – which is a misunderstanding – but the signification of a limitless love which is quite different. The signification of a limitless love, as the end of the analysis represents in its varieties, is precisely the absolute sacrifice.
>
> (p.280)

However, Soler does not differentiate between sacrifice and renunciation. Sacrifice is done on the altar of the ego (a form of idolatry—*Avoda Zara,* a

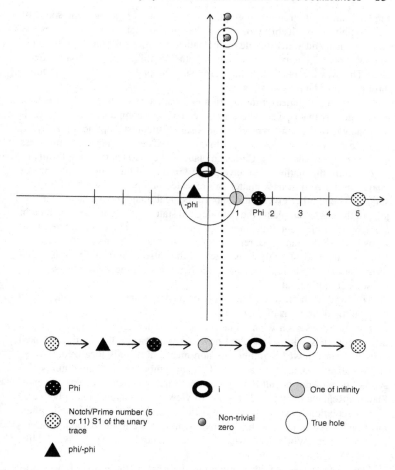

*Graph 7* The complex plane, true and false holes, and prime numbers. This graph shows a simplified complex plane and the critical line and -phi.

form of forbidden service). Renunciation benefits self and other alike, neither an ego sacrifice nor sacrificing the Other. The diamond sutra says there is nobody doing the saving, and nobody being saved, while they are both radically saved.

## Conclusions

This appendix presents Romanowisz's and Moncayo's mathematical theory of the complex plane applied to the Psyche. Something that neither Freud nor

Jung did, although Freud used graph theory, a form of topology, and spoke of the plasticity or malleability of the psyche and the analytic frame. It presents both a logical and a measurable mathematical functions for the Mind/Psyche. This is a revolutionary method that is both scientific and psychoanalytic at once. This way it is possible to measure a singular path for every subject going through life and a personal analysis.

The quantifying measuring function is revealed in two ways. The true hole and the infinity that is everywhere are revealed in the complex plane in the critical zone where the non-trivial zeros or positive Buddhist emptiness is revealed in the i axis of the complex plane, while the trivial zeros or negative emptiness of absence is revealed in the Cartesian plane of the x axis in the complex plane.

Quantum fluctuations that have gravity in the void despite the absence of matter, in the void of dark matter, are revealed in a precise number for every subject. The number gives a measure of the health and mental state of a subject. In the Cartesian plane, the pathological state of the subject is revealed in a precise measurement of the mental pathology of the subject. Negative trivial zeros in the Cartesian x axi, represent for us a measurement of pathology.

When the end of analysis is reached, the false hole of absence is transformed into a true hole representing the emptiness of the Third jouissance of the subject of the Real.

This way we believe we have truly arrived at both a scientific and a psychoanalytic definitions of the cure.

For future research what remains is how to measure two things. We can measure anxiety with a scale, but how can we measure the signifiers linked to anxiety, or can we? Signifiers are non-measurable, only localized, written, and vocalized. So, are we back to a Jungian symbol rather than a number? A symbol here means occult Pythagorean non-mathematical speculation versus Platonic Real mathematics. This point of view implies a rejection of both esoteric speculation (idealism) and simplistic quantification (realism). Signifiers must be ranked in relationship to anxiety, much like in the behavioral treatment of anxiety. With Lacan, what we have is a number and not a symbol like in Jung. A signifier is a number.

Now what happens with numbers in the Real of the i axis? Is it simply that they are de-charged and emptied out to a degree that could be measured? The signifier and the Name become something else in the Real. But this is a qualitative effect. The quantitative effect in subjectivity and psychoanalysis is an experience of jouissance, either in the form of suffering or happiness, that could also be measured as quantum fluctuations that can be measured around a point of absolute zero. Would we gain something if we gave subjects a score for their degree of realization? This would be the correct hierarchical rank order. Out of chaos and disorder, order. We obtain a measure of sublime events: for example, studying art, meditation, yoga, exercise, religion and spirituality, the life of the intellect, and the compassion of the heart.

Meditating one or six times a week gives us a measure of the will and of the number of rebirths of the subject. For the first life the will is weak and instinctual or archaic; for the second rebirth, the will is stronger and enters the practice of meditation, study, or prayer. For the third rebirth, the human subject realizes enlightenment and emptiness.

Although rank-ordered signifiers are mathematically organized by prime numbers, rather than occult numbers and symbols (*Gematria*, numerology), they are not "arithmetized" under *Principia Mathematica*. Numbers here serve the Platonic imperative that science and theory be modelled after mathematics but is not necessarily computational. This is in contrast to "personalizing" and humanizing theory (humanistic psychoanalysis), something that otherwise psychoanalytic treatment cannot avoid.

In "subjective science" and "objective religion", the person or ego is an imaginary description at the level of the theory. In analysis we conceptualize the subject as a metaphor rather than a thing like the ego. The subject is a metaphor, or a number descriptive not of the ego but of a form of jouissance: a Real ego. The Real subject is not an aggregate of signifiers but a form of jouissance. The Third jouissance is like the secondary process in Freud, except that it is primary and ancient. It is a subject in a reduced energetic state which does not mean he/she does not have or use energy, just like the atom is small, yet contains an enormous amount of energy. The Real subject acquires the energy of the vacuum, whether they know it or not.

## References

Dor, J. (1997). *Introduction to the Reading of Lacan. The Unconscious Structured Like Language*. New York: The Other Press.

Erickson, C. (2005). *A Geometric Perspective on the Riemann Zeta Function's Partial Sums*. Mathematics. https://studylib.net/doc/7952796/a-geometric-perspective-on-the-riemann-zeta-function-s-pa; accessed May 23, 2023.

Lacan, J. (1957–1958). *The Seminar of Jacques Lacan V: The Formations of the Unconscious*, unofficial translation by Cormac Gallagher. London: Karnac.

Lacan, J. (1958a). *The Direction of the Treatment and the Principles of Its Power*. Ecrits. A Selection, trans. A. Sheridan, pp.226–280. New York: Norton, 1977.

Soler, C. (2006). *What Lacan Said about Women: A Psychoanalytic Study*, trans. John Holland. Published by New York: Other Press.

## Websites

Graph 1 – Adapted from http://www.maths.surrey.ac.uk/hostedsites/R.Knott/Fibonacci/propsOfPhi.html; accessed on January 24, 2014.

Graph of the Complex Plane. Adapted from Erickson C. (2005). Primary Source Weisstein, Eric W. "Complex Plane." From MathWorld – A Wolfram Web Resource. http://mathworld.wolfram.com/ComplexPlane.html; accessed on January 24, 2014.

Graph on the Critical Line. Adapted from Erickson C., (2005). Primary Source Weisstein, Eric W. "Critical Line." From MathWorld – A Wolfram Web Resource. http://mathworld.wolfram.com/CriticalLine.html; accessed on January 24, 2014.

Graph on the Critical Strip from Erickson C., (2005). Primary Source Weisstein, Eric W. "Critical Strip." From MathWorld – A Wolfram Web Resource. http://mathworld.wolfram.com/CriticalStrip.html; accessed on January 24, 2014.

Graph on Zeros in the Zeta Function. Adapted from website http://mathworld.wolfram.com/RiemannZetaFunctionZeros.html; accessed on January 24, 2014.

Shakespeare, W. Tempest. http://shakespeare.mit.edu/tempest/full.html; accessed on January 24, 2014.

# Glossary

For this entry I relied on three sources: Evans' Dictionary of Lacanian psychoanalysis, Braunstein's "*El Goce: Un Concepto Lacaniano*", and Leader's Jouissance. Leader's book argues that jouissance is merely a descriptive, not a psychoanalytic concept, and as a psychoanalytic concept its ability to stimulate further research is disappointing. He states that Lacanians use the term in an idiosyncratic way as referring mostly to pleasure as the French terms seems to indicate. Leader also reduces Lacan's concept of feminine jouissance to the patriarchal prejudices and cliches that reduce femininity to an enigma (Friedan, 1963). The point of Lacanian research is not to prove to self and other that Lacan was right about everything, but precisely as Leader states, to continue the work that Lacan opened for us. Leader's book is a good reference to find the references to jouissance in Freud's work.

The French word jouissance means basically "enjoyment", but it has a sexual connotation (i.e., "orgasm") lacking in the English word "enjoyment" and is therefore left untranslated in most English editions of Lacan. However, the concept of jouissance also means pain or suffering, a connotation contained in the meaning of the French word. The term does not appear in Lacan's work until 1953 (E, 42, 87). The term seems to mean no more than the enjoyable sensation that accompanies the satisfaction of a biological need such as hunger (S4, 125). However, the sexual connotations of the term would become more apparent. In 1957, Lacan uses the term to refer to the enjoyment of a sexual object (Ec, 453) and to the pleasures of masturbation (S4, 241), and in 1958, he makes explicit the sense of jouissance as orgasm (Ec, 727).

Against Freud's initial simplistic conception of the pleasure principle, the concept of jouissance develops the notion of the pleasure principle as a limit to enjoyment rather than as the drive for pleasure. The experience of satisfaction translates to a lowering of tension, as well as the impossibility of returning to a mythical moment of union with the mother's breast. This eventually produces a connection between the search for pleasure and an increase of tension. Insofar as the pleasure principle functions as a limit to enjoyment, it is a law which commands the subject to "enjoy as little as possible".

The subject, nonetheless, constantly attempts to transgress the prohibitions imposed on his enjoyment, that is, to go "beyond the pleasure principle". However, the result of transgressing the pleasure principle is not more pleasure but pain, since there is only a certain amount of pleasure that the subject can bear. Beyond this limit, pleasure becomes pain, and this "painful pleasure" is what Lacan calls jouissance, "jouissance is suffering" (S7, 184). The term jouissance thus nicely expresses the paradoxical satisfaction that the subject derives from his symptom or, to put it another way, the suffering that he derives from his own satisfaction (Freud's "primary gain from illness").

In his lecture at the Catholic University of Louvain in the 1970s, Lacan asked his audience whether they could bear the life that they had. This question refers to jouissance by pointing to the impossible experience of bearing the unbearable. In this sense, jouissance is intrinsically related to suffering, and not just to pleasure or enjoyment, or even sexuality, as the word commonly refers to in the French language. It is this paradoxical aspect of the drives and of pain and pleasure that is at the core of the definition of jouissance.

In the *Ecrits*, Lacan introduces the concept of jouissance as something inconvenient, deadly, and traumatic that breaks the shield and barrier setup by the pleasure principle to protect the subject from unpleasant and painful experiences. When the protective barrier is breached, or when tensions reach a certain magnitude or threshold, the subject experiences pain rather than pleasure.

At the same time, jouissance not only represents the point where pleasure turns into unpleasure. Jouissance is also used by Lacan to represent a form of phallic enjoyment as a form of pleasure or satisfaction. Lacan speaks of penile and clitoral masturbatory jouissance, for example, as a form of satisfaction involving having or not having the imaginary phallus. Phallic jouissance in this example can also be unpleasant due to the imaginary narcissistic identifications associated with "having" or "not-having" the imaginary phallus.

The jouissance of the Other represents the fusion with the mother and the fantasy of the imaginary phallus. The fusion with the mother is initially necessary, but at some point, it becomes inconvenient without the intervention of the Other that turns the jouissance of the Other into phallic jouissance. Phallic jouissance is pleasant and convenient, so long as it is ruled by symbolic castration. If the phallus remains in an imaginary fantasized position and becomes reified, this leads to an endless search for surplus phallic jouissance that eventually also becomes inconvenient or destructive (as seen in the examples of Don Juan or *la femme fatale*).

If the fantasy of the inexistent imaginary phallus drives the search for surplus jouissance, then revealing the inexistence of imaginary phallus allows the symbolic phallus to function as an organizing principle of the Symbolic. This, in turn, gives access to the Real as the outside the signifier (lack of a signifier for the Real). The symbolic phallus is the signifier of a lack rather than a positive privilege. This is where we witness how Lacan begins to point out the benevolent aspects of the Third jouissance beyond the phallus. What generates this transformation is something internal to the phallic function of castration that both permits and forbids phallic jouissance and causes a movement beyond it.

In Lacan's early work, the inconvenient jouissance is presented in two ways. First, as a deadly excitation that overcomes the protective barriers setup by the pleasure principle and becomes a surplus or excess jouissance. And second, as the malevolent fusion of the mother and the child, when the child occupies the place of the mother's imaginary phallus. The jouissance of the Other between the Real and the Imaginary is an inconvenient jouissance/ pleasure because it is impossible to return to the fusion with the mother. The imaginary One with the mother is the Other that does not exist, rather than the One that "ex-sists" in the Real (*Il y a de l'Un*—There is something of the One). There is no Other of the Other because there is no ideal Other, only greater or lesser approximations. Lacan opens and reconceives this lack in the Other as the Real within the Symbolic. In Seminar XXI "...*Ou pire* (or worse)", Lacan (1971–1972) speaks of the primacy of the One in the register of the Real rather than the Imaginary.

If the first form of jouissance emerges between the Imaginary and the Symbolic as jouissance of the Other, the jouissance Lacan locates between the Symbolic and the Real is a second form referred to as phallic jouissance. Lacan links it to the *parletre* or the speaking being and a parasitic form of power. Phallic jouissance is also a surplus or excessive jouissance that, like a foreign organism, threatens to destroy the psychic body with a preoccupation with the bad infinity of the phi as an irrational number. In phallic jouissance, there is always a calculation with the power of who has or does not have the phallus. Thus, the function of castration and of nomination of the capital Phi, as a Name rather than a number, is required to put a stop to the parasitic bad infinity of the imaginary phallus.

There must be a Third jouissance beyond the jouissance of the Other and phallic jouissance that would correspond to the new definition of the Real that Lacan advances in Seminar XXIII. Lacan began to formulate this Third jouissance in his very dense and abstruse paper *La Trosieme* (1975). However, he did not arrive at a clear formulation of the nature of this Third jouissance.

The relationship between *lalangue* and jouissance is ambiguous in Lacan. *Lalangue* produces what Lacan calls "Other-jouissance" or "jouissance of the Other". The use of the term Other jouissance is not clear in Lacan's work and often is found confused with the jouissance of the Other. Granted, Lacan, as Miller and others have pointed out, often was not clear himself about the six or eight names (rather than concepts) he used for the different types of jouissance. Compare, for example, the definitions given in Seminar XX and "*La troisième*". In Seminar XX, there are two jouissances although the concepts used there imply three jouissances.

"La ***Troisième***" as the title indicates, is dedicated to what we can refer to as the Third jouissance. Here, a Third jouissance is developed from his concept of lalangue and the jouissance of meaning. While the second jouissance is generally recognizable as phallic jouissance, the first and the third are often confused. The jouissance of the Other, or the first jouissance, refers to the inconvenient drive to be an imaginary One with the mother. The Other jouissance, or the Third jouissance, instead refers to feminine jouissance and the jouissance of the mystic (of seminar XX). The Third jouissance presumes the existence of phallic jouissance and the intervention of the paternal and symbolic function.

As well, in Seminar XXIII, Lacan gives us another figure of the Third jouissance he refers to as "*Jouis-sense*", which has been translated as the jouissance of meaning or enjoy-"meant". These three jouissances – of *Jouis-sense*, the feminine, and the mystic, are beyond the phallus.

## References

Friedan, B. (1963). *The Feminine Mystique*. New York: Norton.
Lacan, J. (1972–1973). *Encore*. New York: Norton.
Lacan, J. (1972–1973). *Ou pire* (or worse). http://www.lacaninireland.com/web/translations/seminars. Accessed June 2, 2023.

# Index

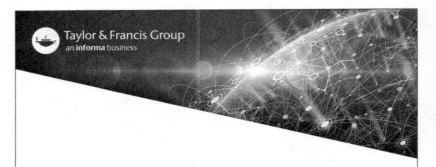

Printed in the United States
by Baker & Taylor Publisher Services